To Persevere in Love

To Persevere in Love

Meditations on the Ministerial Priesthood
from an Anglican Perspective

LEANDER S. HARDING

WIPF & STOCK · Eugene, Oregon

TO PERSEVERE IN LOVE
Meditations on the Ministerial Priesthood from an Anglican Perspective

Copyright © 2013 Leander S. Harding. All rights reserved. Except for brief quotations in critical publications or reviews, no part of this book may be reproduced in any manner without prior written permission from the publisher. Write: Permissions, Wipf and Stock Publishers, 199 W. 8th Ave., Suite 3, Eugene, OR 97401.

Wipf & Stock
An Imprint of Wipf and Stock Publishers
199 W. 8th Ave., Suite 3
Eugene, OR 97401
www.wipfandstock.com

ISBN 13: 978-1-62032-269-7
Manufactured in the U.S.A.

All Scripture quotations are taken from the Holy Bible, Authorized (King James) Version.

Chapter 13, "The Priesthood and the Center," was originally published as "The Ministry and the Center" in *Story Lines: Chapters on Thought, Word, and Deed: For Gabriel Fackre*, eds Fackre and Gibson (Grand Rapids: Eerdmans, 2002). Reprinted with the permission of the Wm. B. Eerdmans Publishing Company.

Chapter 7, "The Power and Dignity of the Priesthood," and chapter 8, "What Have We Been Telling Ourselves about the Priesthood?" appeared in the *Sewanee Theological Review* 43.2 (Easter 2000). Reprinted with the permission of the editor of *Sewanee Theological Review*.

In memory of
Fr. R.A. Watson
Priest, Missionary, Mentor

Contents

Preface ix
Acknowledgments xi

1 Ordination to the Diaconate 1

2 Are Anglican Presbyters Priests? 8

3 Priesthood and Revelation 23

4 The Priesthood and Glory 33

5 The Priesthood and Doctrine 44

6 The Priesthood and Sacrifice 59

7 The Power and Dignity of the Priesthood 67

8 What Have We Been Telling Ourselves about the Priesthood? 76

9 The Good Shepherd 101

10 The Priesthood and Angelic Failure and Angelic Joy 107

11 The Priest, Conversion, and Social Justice 111

12 What Do the Clergy Need to Know? 119

13 The Priesthood and the Center 125

14 On Being a Priest in a Difficult Time 132

15 Are Ordinations and Celebrations of New Ministry Too Elaborate? 138

16 Ontology or Function?: Thoughts on the Anniversary of My Ordination 144

17 Administering the Ashes on Ash Wednesday 2009 148

18   The Priesthood and Parish Conflict   150

19   What is the Essence of the Episcopacy?   155

20   Godly Bishops   158

21   Bearing the Word of God   163

Bibliography   165

Preface

OUR TALK ABOUT MINISTRY and priesthood is oddly imageless, abstract, and generic. We speak of ministry, the ministering community, of facilitating gifts, of empowerment, of spirituality for ministry, of the baptismal covenant, of circles rather than pyramids, of mutuality and mutual ministry, of the Roland Allen model, of mission and the missionary church, of reconciliation, inclusion, justice, and peace. Less often we talk about the Body of Christ and very seldom do we hear of Jesus hanging on the cross, appearing after the Resurrection, breathing upon the disciples, ascending into heaven and there interceding for us as the Great High Priest.

These essays and meditations, some old and some new, are my effort to find the center of the ministry of the priestly people and their ministerial priests in the priesthood of Jesus Christ. I am especially grateful for the encouragement of my colleagues on the faculty of Trinity School for Ministry with whom I have shared conversation and debate about the nature of ordained ministry. The ideas expressed here are my own and influenced by my formation in the more catholic wing of Anglicanism. My hope is that I have been able to teach and write about the range of Anglican views on holy orders in a way that both Evangelical and catholic Anglicans can affirm. It is inevitable that I will not always be equally successful in that aim but I remain committed to the goal of a truly ecumenical theology of holy orders. I am grateful to God for the privilege of teaching in a school that is completely committed to Evangelical essentials but open to students and teachers from both the catholic and charismatic traditions of Anglicanism, and that looks forward to building up the body of Christ in the unity of the faith.

Acknowledgments

I AM GRATEFUL TO Trinity School for Ministry for a sabbatical and to the Conant Fund of The Episcopal Church Foundation for sabbatical funding that allowed me to complete this project. Thanks are also due to Eerdmans Publishing Company and the *Sewanee Theological Review* for permission to republish essays that have appeared in their publications.

1

Ordination to the Diaconate[1]

WE ARE HERE TODAY for the joyous occasion of the ordination of deacons. Beyond and underneath that we are here today because we have died and are risen with Jesus Christ the Lord. In him have we found a new life with God and each other, being reconciled to the Father in one body through the cross of Christ.

In the Eastern Orthodox Church there are vestments, *epimanikion*, which are elaborate cuffs which start at the wrist and run up the arms. The purpose of these cuffs is to show that the hands of the priest or bishop who performs the sacramental rites of the church are not the hands of that person but the hands of Christ. Very shortly the Bishop will be the hands of Christ acting in and through His body the church, as the Lord ordains these three men to be deacons in his one holy Catholic and apostolic Church. In this one body the Holy Spirit pours out gifts for ministry and for the building up of the church upon us all. To some is given the calling and gift of ordination.

A sacrament consists of two things: the promise of God and an effectual sign of that promise. When the appropriate and appointed sign is brought together with the proclamation of God's promise, the God who fulfills his promises is present and active in our midst. In the case of ordination the sign is a person set apart by prayer and the laying on of hands for ordained service in the church. The promise that is being kept is the promise of the Lord that he would not desert us but would be with us always even to the end of the age (Matt 28:20). The vocation of the church is to

---

1. Sermon preached at Trinity Cathedral, Pittsburgh, Pennsylvania, June 2, 2012.

be the body of Christ, Christ's hands and feet and speech and touch in the world. The vocation of the clergy is to make Christ present to his people in such a way that the life of Christ is stirred up in them and they constantly rediscover that they are alive only insofar as they live in Him and He lives in them.

The great Anglican theologian Austin Farrar said in an ordination sermon that the clergy are walking sacraments. The role of the clergy, the life to which they are irrevocably committed is to be effectual signs of Christ working in his church, making his people his own, and making them potent witnesses of the salvation he has come to bring.

It is tempting to think of ordination in terms drawn from the world around us. Someone studies the law and then passes the bar and therefore enters the legal profession. There comes a moment when they are authorized to practice law. Someone studies medicine and is granted the medical degree, then passes the boards and is therefore authorized to practice medicine. We can think of similar rites of passage in the world of business and in other professions and vocations. In this political season the image of the election is before us and we can be tempted to think of the candidate who is elected and then inaugurated into his or her office. Necessarily there are echoes of all these things in an ordination. The candidates have had to complete a course of study. They have been tried and examined. They will, after their ordination, be inaugurated into a particular office in the church by those with the authority to give them that office. If they go to a parish there may well be an element of election about it.

All this is meet and right. But these things are not the essence of holy orders. The holy orders of the church depend ultimately on the mysterious calling and grace of God. There is no question of anyone having a right to be ordained or deserving to be ordained. God calls the few for the sake of the salvation of the many. And the few that he calls have as their main qualification an understanding that they are nothing in themselves. Their main qualification is that they know themselves to be the recipients of a costly and undeserved forgiveness. I am always a little worried by the call which goes out every now and then to recruit for the church's service the "best and the brightest". To the extent that the persons being recruited understood themselves to be "the best and the brightest" would be precisely the extent to which they were disqualified for ordained service. God can use all sorts of people in the ordained ministry including the best and the brightest as

Ordination to the Diaconate

long as they understand with St. Paul that they hold the treasure of this ministry in earthen vessels.

This is true of the whole church. We have been called out of the world and have been elected by God to be his witnesses and to bring the word of his sacrificial love to all his lost children. We certainly have not been called because we are especially virtuous or especially religious or especially deserving in any way. Before Christ we recognize ourselves as people who have turned away from God, turned on each other, and turned in on ourselves. Before Christ we recognize ourselves as the undeserving enemies of God to whom he has come in the person of his Son and in the face of our hatred and rejection and murder to bring us the love of God. Before Christ we recognize ourselves as those who drive the Son of God out of the world and onto the cross. To recognize these things is to die and at the same time to be put in the place where it is possible to receive the abundant and eternal life that the Savior brings forth from the grave. We have been elected to be recipients of the undeserved love of God that we might be witnesses of this love to a world which is estranged from its creator, and to continue the ministry of the Savior to reconcile all people to his Father, and as the old prayer book says, "to seek for Christ's sheep that are dispersed abroad, and for his children who are in the midst of this naughty world, that they may be saved through Christ forever."

Within the one body of Christ, which is an elect and ordained people, there are those who are called out and ordained to the holy orders of the church. It is their calling to represent to the whole church in a special way its utter dependence upon the One who is its head. It is their calling to keep alive at the heart of the church the animating image of the Lord as prophet, priest, and king, who came not to be served but to serve. The great Orthodox theologian and priest Alexander Schmemann famously said that the reason why a man is ordained a priest is not because some men are more holy than others but so that all men can be recalled to their vocation.

The Bishop is a living reminder to us that we are here because the word of God has come to us through his apostles, through the messengers whom he ordained and sent. The Bishop reminds us by his living witness as an ordained person that the whole body is dependent upon its one head and upon the death and resurrection of its Lord. The one hundredth Archbishop of Canterbury, Michael Ramsey, loved to explain the mystery of the church by quoting 2 Corinthians 5:14, "One died for all therefore all died." And through that death have we been born anew.

To Persevere in Love

When I was ordained a deacon more than thirty-one years ago on a cold December night, the Bishop, when it was time to actually perform the ordination, removed his cope and put on four sets of vestments. First the tunicle of the laity, then the deacon's dalmatic, then the chasuble of the priest and then another chasuble representing the high priesthood of the episcopate. The purpose of the moment was to show that the Bishop had in himself the fullness of the apostolic ministry as the one who represents the Lord sending others in his stead. "As the Father has sent me, I also send you" (John 20:21).

According to the guidance of the Holy Spirit over time, the bishops, who are the successors of the apostles, have delegated some aspects of their ministry to deacons and priests. Priests share with them in the administration of baptism and the celebration of the Eucharist and the pastoring of the flock of Christ. Deacons are given a special responsibility for the poor, the sick, and the lonely, and assist the bishop and the priests in the preaching of the word of God and the administration of the sacraments. The reason why some people are ordained to the diaconate is not because some people are more holy than others but so that the call to servanthood to the whole church can be kept alive at the heart of the church by an ordained icon of Jesus Christ who came not to be served but to serve. One is called so that many may be called.

Whenever we cast our eyes upon the deacon and especially when the deacon reads the gospel in the Eucharist, we are meant to think of Jesus in the synagogue at Nazareth reading the scroll of the prophet Isaiah and saying "the Spirit of the Lord is upon me because he has called me to preach good news to the poor" (Luke 4:18). Whenever we cast our eyes upon the deacon we are meant to see our Lord girding himself with a towel and washing the feet of his disciples on the night in which he is betrayed and given up to death. The deacon is a walking sacrament and a living icon of Christ the servant present in the midst of his people stirring them up to servanthood. Just here there is a temptation, and that is to think about the servant Christ apart from his death and resurrection. The concern of Jesus Christ for the poor, his proclamation of liberty, his works of feeding and healing make sense to the world. His cross and resurrection, which confound the wisdom of this world and judge the wickedness and sin of the human race and in just that moment open the way of resurrection, salvation, and eternal life, are nonsense to the world. In the words of St. Paul, "the cross of Jesus Christ is foolishness to Greeks and a stumbling block to

Jews but to us who are being saved it is the power of God and the wisdom of God" (1 Cor 1:18).

There is a natural human temptation that is in no way new to have Jesus the prophet of justice and the worker of healing without his cross and resurrection. It is a desire to find righteousness for ourselves by finding righteous victims and having some of that righteousness rub off on us. It is an attempt to escape the judgment of the cross. In the nineteenth century this was called the religion of the fatherhood of God and the brotherhood of man. It is a thinned out version of Christianity which reduces the mystery of the crucified and risen Savior to the teaching of a good man who encourages good works. In our own time we can recognize versions of the Christian faith that so focus on the mercy and fellowship of the Lord in Galilee that the cross of Calvary and the miraculous resurrection which follows drop out of sight.

The holy orders of the Church are the gift of the crucified, risen, and ascended Lord to his Church. The order of the diaconate is a special form of the presence of Jesus the servant in the midst of his servant people. But it must be always seen that the one who cast out the demons, who healed the sick, who fed the hungry and proclaimed good news to the poor was on his way to die that we might live. The deacon who will authentically carry the charism of the order will be a witness not only to the charitable deeds of Christ but also to his saving death and mighty resurrection. This is only possible as we know ourselves as people who have died and whose life is hid with God in Christ.

It is a vastly important part of our witness to Jesus Christ that the hungry are fed, the naked are clothed, the sick are healed, and the poor have good news preached to them. But if we do not bring Christ near to them in proclamation and in witness in such a way that they too can be reconciled to the Father in one body through the cross, then in the end we have left them still hungry, starving for the word of God, naked, still clothed in the rags of sin, and without the healing that really matters and compared with which all other healings are temporary, and that is the healing of the rift between the Father and his children which is the only hope for peace for this world and life in the world to come. If we have relieved only their this-worldly needs, we have not shared the good news of the new life with God and with each other, which begins now and which the grave cannot hold. The ordained person proclaims this good news in teaching and preaching and in acts of service, but also because they themselves have died with

Christ and been born anew from above, and it is evident as much by who they are as by what they say.

One of the really good things that have happened in the time that I have been ordained has been a growing appreciation for the sacramental sign of the diaconate in the church. A great deal has been done to restore the dignity of the order of deacons in the life of the church. Some have proposed that to give the diaconate its proper significance, the practice of ordaining persons to what is not very happily called the transitional diaconate should be discontinued. I say that "transitional diaconate" is an unhappy phrase because I do not regard my diaconate as a transition. I haven't transited out of being a deacon. I'm still a deacon. And deep in the heart of my priesthood is buried, in the way that a deep foundation is buried, my ordination as a deacon.

Some argue for what are called *per saltum* ordinations. That means ordaining somebody in a jump. So those that are destined for ordination as priests would cease to be ordained as deacons. Even more radically that someone could be ordained from the lay order to the episcopate in a jump. I think this would be a mistake. I believe, as did the Bishop who ordained me, that the greater orders contain the lesser ones within them. But the ladder goes up as well as down. I also think that in the upside down logic of the Gospel that the lesser order of the diaconate is indispensable to the order of priest and the order of bishop. The greater orders of priest and bishop contain within them like a beating heart the order of the diaconate. The priesthood and the episcopacy include increased responsibilities and increased authorities. The priest and the bishop do not have the luxury of caring only for the poor, the sick, and the lonely. They must care for the whole flock. They must carry the icon, not only of Christ the servant but more comprehensively and more clearly the icon of Christ the prophet, priest, and king or ruler. But all of these roles, if they are to be authentic and adequate to the Lord who bequeaths them to the church through the apostolic ministry, must be rooted and grounded in the spirit of Christ the servant. Priesthood and episcopacy which are not at the same time profoundly diaconal miss the inner secret of their charism.

The great Christian virtue is the virtue of humility. Christ humbled himself that we might be exalted. The authentic Christian minister is the one who has been humbled at the foot of the cross. That humility, which leads to joy and gratitude and service, is the foundation of the priesthood of all believers and of the special priesthood of the ordained. It is very meet

Ordination to the Diaconate

and right that those who are being called ultimately to be priests and pastors should begin by being so clearly ordained to be icons of humble service.

My prayer for you as you come to be ordained is that you will completely surrender your selves to the grace of ordination and be truly and recognizably walking sacraments of Christ, able to stir up the life of Christ in the people you are called to serve. My prayer is that you will so obviously be people who are humbled by the cross of Christ that the death of Christ is at work through you, and that you are so overwhelmed by the gratuitous love of Christ that the life of the resurrection is at work through you as well. "For we carry about in ourselves the death of Jesus, that the life of Jesus might be made known in us as well" (2 Cor 4:10). Amen.

2

Are Anglican Presbyters Priests?

R.C. Moberly on the Ministerial Priesthood

ANGLICAN ORDINALS HAVE ALWAYS used the terminology of bishop, priest, and deacon. There has been tension within Anglicanism about the meaning of the term "priest." Clearly there was a desire by the English Reformers to distance themselves from what they regarded as a superstitious understanding of the priesthood associated with a view of the Eucharist as a propitiatory sacrifice which crucified Christ anew in every celebration. If this were true, the priesthood was a sacred cadre that had the power to mediate between God and humanity in the place of Christ. This according to Reformation polemic was the horror of the Mass. On the one hand, traditional Anglican theology upholds the priority of justification by grace through faith and the priesthood of all believers, and on the other affirms in the preface to the ordinal that it desires to continue that sacred ministry which the church has always known.[1] At the time of the English Reformation the Puritans promoted Presbyterian order and objected to the term "priest" in the ordinal. Richard Hooker in the *Lawes of Ecclesiastical Polity* defends the use of the term "priest" as simply the English form of the word "presbyter" but then also says that the presbyterate is what the Church has that is "proportionate" to the priesthood of the Old Testament.[2] That icon of the Anglican pastor George Herbert (born 1593) wrote a wonderful poem

---

1. Church of England, *The Book of Common Prayer*.
2. Hooker, *Works of Richard Hooker*.

that is a meditation on the role of the ordained Anglican pastor, which interweaves themes from the doctrine of justification and the priesthood of Aaron.[3] It is a beautiful poem and rich with a properly Anglican spirituality of the ordained ministry. Though the poem is an extended meditation on justification by grace through faith, Herbert has no difficulty using the word priest with allusions to the Old Testament priesthood in his reflection on the spirituality of the Anglican pastor.

> HOLINESSE on the head,
> Light and perfections on the breast,
> Harmonious bells below, raising the dead
> To leade them unto life and rest:
> Thus are true Aarons drest.
>
> Profaneness in my head,
> Defects and darknesse in my breast,
> A noise of passions ringing me for dead
> Unto a place where is no rest:
> Poore priest, thus am I drest.
>
> Onely another head
> I have, another heart and breast,
> Another musick, making live, not dead,
> Without Whom I could have no rest:
> In Him I am well drest.
>
> Christ is my onely head,
> My alone-onely heart and breast,
> My onely musick, striking me ev'n dead;
> That to the old man I may rest,
> And be in Him new-drest.
>
> So, holy in my Head,
> Perfect and light in my deare breast,
> My doctrine tun'd by Christ, Who is not dead,
> But lives in me while I do rest,
> Come, people; Aaron's drest.

3. Herbert, *The Poetical Works of George Herbert*, 218.

Particularly since the tension between Evangelical and Anglo-Catholic church parties in the nineteenth century, Anglican Evangelicals have insisted that the Anglican presbyter is not a priest and that there is no sacerdotal function that is proper to the Anglican understanding of the ordained pastor. This is the source of the traditional Anglican Evangelical objection to Eucharistic vestments. It is thought that chasubles imply an understanding of the Eucharist as a propitiatory re-immolation of Christ conducted by a priesthood that usurps the place of the one mediator. Anglo-Catholics with their emphasis on the divine commission of the church's ordained ministry have quoted the preface to the ordinal in defense of the ministerial priesthood and have sought to uphold an understanding of the ordained as unique (though not exclusive) icons of Christ representing His priesthood in the midst of the church.

The Anglican Evangelical disparagement of the ministerial priesthood of the ordained has had an ally in the official teaching of the Roman Catholic Church. In 1896, Pope Leo XIII issued the Papal Bull *Apostolicae Curae*, declaring Anglican orders, "absolutely null and completely void."[4] The papal bull found both the form and intention of the historic Anglican ordinals defective. According to the bull, Anglicans do not understand the Eucharist as a sacrifice and do not intend to ordain priests since the words of the Anglican ordinal "certainly do not in the least express the Sacred Order of Priesthood, or its grace and power, which is chiefly the power '*of consecrating and offering the true body and blood of the Lord*' (Council of Trent, Sess. XXIII., *de Sacr. Ord.*, Can. 1) in that sacrifice which is no '*nude commemoration of the sacrifice offered on the Cross.*' (Ibid. Sess. XXII., *de Sacrif. Missae. Can. 3).*"[5]

The bull explicitly rebuffs Anglo-Catholic attempts to argue that the ordinal as a whole including the preface and accompanying prayers supports a chastened but real sacerdotal understanding of the priesthood. "In vain those who, from the time of Charles I., have attempted to hold some kind of sacrifice or of priesthood.... In vain also has been the contention of that small section of the Anglican body formed in recent times, that the said Ordinal can be understood and interpreted in a sound and orthodox sense."[6]

---

4. Franklin, *Anglican Orders*, 136. This very helpful volume has the English text of the Papal bull and the English text of the Latin reply *Saepius Officio* by the Archbishops of York and Canterbury published in 1897.

5. Ibid., Section 8, 134.

6. Ibid., 134.

Are Anglican Presbyters Priests?

Evangelical Anglicans who opposed the association of any sacerdotal vocabulary with the ministry of Anglican presbyters, any mention of ministerial priesthood or the offering of sacrifice in connection with the pastorate, were bolstered by the bull.

The Archbishops of York and Canterbury answered *Apostolicae Curae* with a learned and irenic letter entitled *Saepius Officio*,[7] "addressed to the whole body of Bishops of the Catholic Church," which implied Anglican, Roman Catholic, and Orthodox bishops. The Archbishops acknowledge that there was sensitivity to the language of priesthood and sacrifice in the compilation of the Edwardian ordinal in section XIX.[8] Yet they also in speaking about the high priesthood of the episcopacy say, "although in our Ordinal we say nothing about high Priests and Pontiffs, we do not avoid using the terms in other public documents. Examples may be taken from the Latin edition of the *Book of Common* Prayer, AD 1560, from the letter written by twelve Bishops on behalf of Archbishop Grindall, AD 1580, and from Archbishop Whitgift's Commission to his Suffragan the Bishop of Dover, AD 1583."[9]

The Archbishops assert in a matter of fact way that "Bishops are undoubtedly Priests, just as Presbyters are Priests."[10] With regard to the Papal swipe at Anglo-Catholic interpretation of the Anglican ordinal, the archbishops reply that,

> the intention of our Church, not merely of a newly formed party in it, is quite clearly set forth in the title and preface of the Ordinal. The title in 1552 ran "The fourme and manner of makynge and consecratynge Bishoppes, Priestes and Deacons." The preface immediately following begins thus: "It is euident unto all men, diligently reading holye Scripture and aunciert aucthours, that from the Apostles tyme there hathe bene these ordres of Ministers in Christ's Church: Bishoppes, Priestes, and Deacons: which Offices were euermore had in suche reurent estimacion, that no man by his own private aucthoritie might presume to execute any of them, except he were first called, tried, examined, and knowen to have such qualities as were requisite for the same; And also, by publique prayer, with imposicion of hands, approued, and admitted thereunto. And therfore, to the entent that these orders shoulde bee

---

7. Ibid., 138.
8. Ibid., 147. Section XIX of *Saepius Officio*.
9. Ibid, 144. XII of *SO*.
10. Ibid., 144.

continued, and reuerentlye used and esteemed, in this Church of England; ...". ... Thus the intention of our Fathers was to keep and continue these offices which come down from the earliest times, and "reverently to use and esteem them," in the sense, of course, in which they were received from the Apostles and had been up to that time in use. This is a point on which the Pope is unduly silent."[11]

The Archbishops accuse the Roman Pontifical rite of ordination then in use of over-emphasizing the offering of the Eucharist at the expense of other elements of the priesthood and assert that the Anglican is a more balanced presentation of the office, "inasmuch as it expresses more clearly and faithfully those things which by Christ's institution belong to the nature of the priesthood (part 9) and the effect of the Catholic rites used in the Universal Church."[12]

In the official reply of the Archbishops of York and Canterbury to Leo XIII's denunciation of the validity of Anglican orders, the Anglican ambivalence about the nomenclature of sacrifice and priesthood is in full view. A reserve about using this sacerdotal vocabulary is defended lest it encourage false views of the nature of the real presence in the Eucharist, the nature of Eucharistic sacrifice, and the nature of the priesthood. Yet the use of the word sacrifice referring to the Eucharist and priesthood referring to both the presbyterate and the episcopacy are retained and defended. It also is vigorously maintained that the Anglican Church has ever intended to maintain the same holy orders which the church has had from the time of the Apostles and which is shared with the ecumenical church including the Greek Orthodox.[13]

In 1897 one of the classic books on the topic of Anglican orders was published by Robert Campbell Moberly, D.D. Moberly, born in 1845, was the son of the bishop of Salisbury and the first principal of the Anglo-Catholic theological college, St. Stephen's House, and later Regius Professor of Pastoral Theology, Oxford, and Canon of Christ Church. His book, *Ministerial Priesthood. Chapters (preliminary to a Study of the Ordinal) on the Rationale of Ministry and the Meaning of Christian Priesthood with an Appendix Upon Roman Criticism of Anglican Orders*,[14] quickly went through two editions

11. Ibid., 144–145. XIII of *SO*.
12. Ibid., 146. XIX of *SO*.
13. Ibid., 148. XX of *SO*.
14. Moberly, *Ministerial Priesthood*.

Are Anglican Presbyters Priests?

and provoked a vigorous debate in the Church of England including with the great New Testament scholar J.B. Lightfoot.[15] The book became one of the standard texts on ordained ministry in Anglican theological colleges with a catholic orientation. The copy I drew out of our seminary library to consult has the name of a cleric I knew well when I was first ordained. The book was clearly his textbook on Anglican orders at General Theological Seminary in New York City. The date given in the student's hand is 1952. This is anecdotal evidence of the long service of Moberly's book especially in the American setting. Moberly's book is, I believe, a careful, irenic, and scholarly consideration of the fraught topic of ministerial priesthood in the Anglican context. The book is a product of its time and the times have changed. Nevertheless what he says about ministerial priesthood has an enduring quality and holds up a vision of the ordained ministry which is appropriately evangelical and catholic. I also believe that Moberly's views on ministerial priesthood stand up very well to current ecumenical reflections on the topic.

Moberly recognized that there was good reason for the reticence about the language of sacrifice and priesthood in the Edwardian Ordinal. The mass was often seen at least in the popular mind as "an outward performance of intrinsic efficacy, to be so many times repeated with the value arithmetically calculable; and so that the Priest stood as a real intermediary between the *plebs Christiana* and its God, to make, by sacrifice, atonement for sin."[16]

Moberly identified two false options. The radical Protestant option was to sweep away altogether the language of priesthood and sacrifice. The Roman option was to keep the language as altogether right and rightly proportioned. In Moberly's view the Anglican ordinal chose neither false option. The Anglican ordinal sought not to utterly sweep away the language of sacrifice and priesthood but to put it in proper proportion. "What they did clearly implies (1) that they did not judge it wholly wrong nomenclature, and (2) that its conception and statement had nevertheless, in their eyes, so far fallen out of due proportion as, if not to contradict, yet at least to jeopardize, the right balance of Christian truth."[17]

---

15. Lightfoot, *Dissertations on the Apostolic Age*. Lightfoot had appended a twenty-five page appendix to this work attacking sacerdotal language applied to ordained ministry, and Moberly was at pains to take up Lightfoot's objections in his own work.

16. Moberly, *Ministerial Priesthood*, 221.

17. Ibid., 234.

While grateful that the Anglican reformers resisted doing away altogether with the terminology of priesthood despite "a simple ferocity" of opposition to it, he saw continuing danger that proper use of the language suffered from both the Roman Catholic and Evangelical sides. Bishop Lightfoot, in the last twenty-five pages of his book on the Apostolic age, made a vigorous argument against the use of what he called "sacerdotal" language.[18] Moberly thought that Lightfoot had been misled by his preconceptions about the nature of priesthood.

> It is plain from these passages that Bishop Lightfoot has (1) made the capital mistake of taking the Mosaic use of the words "priesthood," &c. as the truth and true standard of their meaning, and measuring, by that, their meaning in the Church of Christ: and (2) that he has gone on from this initial—and fatal—mistake, to allow himself to consider (a) the sacrifice is so spoken of as things in themselves independent and absolute—as actual offerings of atonement; and so (B) the priests as a class really intervening, as indispensable intermediaries, between Christians and their God. Thus he speaks of priests as a "sacerdotal caste" "in some exclusive sense" (to which the idea of his standing to represent the congregation is regarded as antithetical), as "an exclusive priesthood"; of their claim to "sacerdotal privileges" and "sacerdotal sanctity" (phrases which are not explained); of their claim to "obedience" on pain of profanity and sacrilege; and again, by implication at least, of their being sacerdotal, and the Eucharist as a sacerdotal act, "in the same sense in which the Jewish priesthood and the Jewish sacrifices were sacerdotal"; of their "vicarial" character—regarded as antithetical to being "representative"; of the interposing of the priest "between God and man in such a way that direct communication with God is superseded on the one hand, and that his own mediation becomes indispensable on the other." And he not unnaturally concludes by the position that the words themselves can only be retained "in a wider and looser sense" than that which his argument has treated throughout as if it were the one that most properly belonged to them.[19]

According to Moberly the ministerial priesthood is not set over against the church as an intermediary between God and the laity as the whole people of God. Rather the ministerial priesthood exists in and for the Church.

18. Lightfoot, *Dissertations on the Apostolic Age*.
19. Moberly, *Ministerial Priesthood*, 241.

> ... the Christian ministry is not a substituted intermediary—still less an atoning mediator—between God and laypeople; but is rather the representative and organ of the whole body, in the exercise of the prerogatives and powers which belong to the body as a whole. It is ministerially empowered to wield, as the body's organic representative, the powers which belong *to the body*, but which the body cannot wield except through its own organs duly fitted for the purpose. What is duly done by Christian Ministers, it is not so much that *they* do it, in the stead, or for the sake, of the whole; but rather that the whole does it by and through them. The Christian Priest does not offer an atoning sacrifice on behalf of the Church: it is rather the Church through his act that, not so much "offers an atonement," as "is identified upon earth with the one heavenly offering of the atonement of Christ." In light of this one great principle, as I conceive, all that the Bishop says about a sacerdotal caste, its exclusiveness, its intervention, its sacerdotal privileges and sanctity, its demand of obedience on pain of sacrilege, almost, or quite, totally disappears.[20]

Moberly insists that a proper understanding of ministerial priesthood must take its cues from the priesthood of Jesus Christ. "No, there is one standard only, and measure, of the reality of the meaning of these words; that is, their meaning in the Person of Christ."[21] An additional problem arises in understanding the nature of Christ's priesthood which comes from a misunderstanding of the meaning of sacrifice in the Old Testament. Sacrifice is not identical with the death of the victim. It is the offering of the blood that represents life that is truly essential for sacrifice.

> The culminating point of the sacrifice was not in the shedding of the blood, but in the presentation before God, in the holy place, of the blood that had been shed; of the life, that is, which had passed through death, and had been consecrated to God by dying. It is not the death itself which is acceptable to the God of life: but the vital self-identification with the holiness of God, the perfect self-dedication and self-surrender which is represented, in a life that has sinned, by voluntary acceptance of penitential or penal death. It is the life as life, not the death as death; it is the life which has been willing to die, the life which has passed through death, and been consecrated in dying, the life in which death is a

---

20. Ibid., 242.
21. Ibid., 244.

moral element, perpetually and inalienably present, but still *the life*, which is acceptable to God.²²

Moberly believed that the meaning of sacrifice in Eucharistic theology and the understanding of the ministerial priesthood suffered from this confusion between death and sacrifice. This led in the consideration of both terms to an over-emphasis on Calvary at the expense of the Ascension. "Christ's offering in heaven is a perpetual ever-present offering of life, whereof 'to have died' is an ever-present and perpetual attribute. If 'Calvary' were the sufficient statement of the nature of the sacrifice of Christ, then that sacrifice would be simply past and done, which is in truth both now and forever present. He is a Priest forever, not as it were by a perpetual series of acts of memory, not by multiplied and ever remoter acts of commemoration of a death that is past, but by the eternal presentation of a life which eternally is the 'life that died.'"²³

Sacrifice according to Moberly takes the form of crucifixion in the realm of sin. The cross is the result and the consequence of sin. Yet, Moberly says, there must be more to sacrifice than the form it takes under the circumstances of sin. There must be a root of sacrifice that is more fundamental. "What is that which must become sacrifice in sin's atmosphere; and which sacrifice, as it passes beyond sin's atmosphere, is found really to be? There can be no doubt of the answer. It is love. . . . There is no essential contrast between sacrifice and love. Love, under certain disabling conditions, becomes sacrifice; and sacrifice is not sacrifice, except it be love."²⁴

Moberly says that the priesthood of Christ is simply divine love under the conditions of humanity. Christ's priesthood thus has a Godward dimension and a manward dimension. "To manward it is inconceivable condescension and embrace of love, divinely redeeming; to Godward it is the homage, perfect and perpetual—as, primarily, of human penitential atonement for sin—so also of human sinlessness, and unblemished service, and response of love worthy of God."²⁵

Moberly has already argued that whatever Christ is, the Church is. So this priestly sacrifice of Christ overflows into the Church and necessarily determines the character of both the laity understood as the whole people of God and of the Church's ordained ministry.

22. Ibid., 244–245.
23. Ibid., 246.
24. Ibid., 247–248.
25. Ibid., 249–250.

Because sacrifice means love and the priesthood of Christ is His love in action, the priestly dimension of Christ's ministry informs the other dimensions as well. The love that is at the bottom of his sacrifice and priesthood is at the bottom of his prophetic and royal office as well. There is no question of conflict between the prophetic, preaching office and the priestly, liturgical office in the ministerial priesthood or between these and the pastoral ruling office. They are all alike grounded in and shaped by the priestly sacrificial love of Christ. This priestly and sacrificial spirit is the Church's because it is Christ's, and the nomenclature of priesthood belongs properly both to the Church as a whole and to the ordained presbyters because it belongs to Christ whose servants they are, each in their appointed role. Therefore to deprecate the priesthood of the ordained presbyter will inevitably deprecate the priesthood of the priestly people as well. "If this be once conceded and understood, I do not apprehend that much difficulty will remain about the priestly character of the ministry of the church. If those be right to deprecate the use of the words priest and priestly, all substantial reality in the conception of the priesthood of the layman must go too. The priesthood of the ministry is to be established not through deprecation, but through exaltation, of the priesthood of the body as a whole."[26]

For Moberly this spirit of sacrificial divine love finds its essential and indispensable expression in the celebration of the Eucharist. In the Eucharist the whole church as the mystical body of Christ becomes what it truly is by identifying itself with the sacrificial love the Son of God offers to the Father for the sake of humanity and to the human race for the sake of the Father.

> The sacrificial priesthood of the Church is really her identification with the priesthood and sacrifice of Christ. With this priesthood and sacrifice she is identified outwardly and inwardly; by outward enactments ceremonially, and by inwardness of spirit vitally. Christ Himself has prescribed for all time an outward ceremonial, which is the symbolic counterpart in the Church on earth, not simply of Calvary, but of that eternal presentation of Himself in heaven in which Calvary is vitally contained. Through the symbolic enactment, rightly understood, an enactment founded on and intrinsically implying as well as recalling Calvary, she in her Eucharistic worship on earth is identified with His sacrificial self-oblation to the Father; she is transfigured up into the scene of the unceasing commemoration of His sacrifice in heaven; or the scene of His

---

26. Ibid., 254.

> eternal offering in heaven is translated down to, and presented, and realized in the worship on earth.[27]

According to Moberly the ordained priest is not an intermediary and substitute for the mediation of Christ. The ordained priest does not stand over against the church but in and for the Church as its appointed and organic instrument through which the Church recognizes the voice of her master calling her to identify herself with His one sufficient sacrifice which He eternally pleads before the Father.

> For the priesthood of the ministry is nothing distinct in kind from the priesthood of the Church. The ordained priests are priestly only because it is the church's prerogative to be priestly; and because they are, by ordination, specialized and empowered to exercise ministerially and organically the prerogatives which are the prerogatives of the body as a whole. They have no greater right in the Sacraments than the laity: only they, and not the laity, have been authorized to stand before the congregation, and to represent the congregation in the ministerial enactment of the Sacraments which are the Sacraments, and the life, of both alike.[28]

The priesthood of the ordained priest finds its ultimate expression in the leadership of the Eucharistic assembly. The role of liturgical leadership in the Church's worship must, according to Moberly, be understood in such a way that the liturgical function expresses and does not eclipse the whole range of concerns which make up the pastoral ministry. Thus ministerial priesthood properly understood includes within itself a balance of preaching, teaching, pastoring, and administration. The ministerial priesthood also must in all its function be an outward expression of an inner spirituality grounded in the divine love and sacrifice of Christ.

> There are not only priestly functions, or priestly prerogatives: there is also a priestly spirit and a priestly heart—more vital to true reality of priesthood than any mere performance of priestly functions. Now this priestly spirit—I must repeat it once more—is *not* the exclusive possession of the ordained ministry; it is the spirit of the priestly Church. But those who are ordained "priests" are bound to be eminently leaders and representatives of this priestliness of spirit, and they have assigned to them an external sphere and professional duties which constitute a special opportunity,

---

27. Ibid., 255.
28. Ibid., 257–258.

and the charisma of grace which constitutes a special call and a special capacity, for its exercise. Such opportunity and call are inseparable from the oversight of the life of the Christian body to Godward, and they are as wide as is the life of the Christian body. Leadership in Eucharistic worship, truly understood, is its highest typical expression, the mystical culmination of its executive privilege; but Eucharistic leadership, truly understood, involves many corollaries of spirit and life: the bearing of the people on the heart before God; the earnest effort of intercessory entreating; the practical translation of intercession into pastoral life, and anxiety, and pain. Things like these are necessary elements in that inwardness of spirit which should correspond to and explain the outward dignity of executive function; and apart from which the outward dignity of executive function, even in its highest point of mystical reality, is as the shell or the shadow, the outward presentment and image, the technical enacting—not the true heart—of Christian priesthood.[29]

Understanding the ministerial priesthood in this way, Moberly can see no contradiction between the priesthood of all believers and the ordained priesthood and can see no reason why the term priest should not be applied to the ministry of the ordained presbyter.

> It is necessary, then, to emphasize unreservedly the truth that the priesthood of ministry and of laity are not really antithetical or inconsistent, but rather correlative, complementary, nay, mutually indispensable ideas. Magnify first the solemnity of ministerial priesthood, and then from that expound the dignity and power of the priesthood of the laity; or, if you will, magnify lay priesthood first, and mount from thence to its concentrated meaning in those who are set apart personally to represent the collective priesthood, and to wield it ministerially: in either case your exposition will lead to results which will be no less true than they may well be felt to be amazing. But use the phrases "priesthood of the laity" (or "priesthood of the body") in order to discredit the idea of ministerial priesthood; and from ministerial priesthood thus explained away turn to draw out what the universal priesthood practically means; and you will have succeeded, with admirable skill, in conjuring both realities into empty air. It will only remain to toss the whole nomenclature aside, as an unmeaning or misleading metaphor.[30]

29. Ibid., 261.
30. Ibid., 262.

To Persevere in Love

Though Moberly wishes that the Edwardian Ordinal had been more explicit in its use of priestly language with regard to the office of the ordained presbyter, he believes that the Anglican reformers attended carefully to the inner spirit of true Christian priesthood and to the proper balance of all the pastoral functions in the ordained ministry of the church.

> It is then this central meaning, this spiritual inwardness of the office of Church leadership as a whole, which stands in the forefront of the Anglican Ordinal, as that upon which the thought is primarily centered. Throughout that most solemn exhortation addressed to all candidates for priesthood the ring of St. Paul's words in Acts XX is never absent. It is to a "high dignity" to a "weighty office and charge" that they are called; "to be messengers, watchmen, and stewards of the Lord; to teach and to premonish; to feed and provide for the Lord's family; to seek for Christ's sheep that are dispersed abroad, and for His children who are in the midst of this naughty world, that they may be saved through Christ forever. Have always therefore printed in your remembrance how great a treasure is committed to your charge. For they are the sheep of Christ, which He bought with His death, and for whom He shed His Blood. The Church and congregation whom you must serve is His Spouse and His Body. . . . Wherefore consider with yourselves the end of your ministry towards the children of God, towards the Spouse and Body of Christ. . . ." All this is cardinal and primary. But the solemn administration, and discipline, of sacraments, the "binding and loosing," are also emphasized, if no longer as the one thing which Christian priesthood means, yet in their place, in perfect order, as the supreme and typical summing up of all ordinances of outward administration. "Will you give your faithful diligence always so to minister the Doctrine and Sacraments, and the Discipline of Christ, as the Lord hath commanded, and as this Church and Realm hath received the same?". . . "Receive the Holy Ghost [for the office and work of the Priest in the Church of God, now committed unto thee by the imposition of our hands]. Whose sins thou dost forgive, they are forgiven; and whose sins thou dost retain, they are retained. And be thou a faithful dispenser of the Word of God and of His Holy Sacraments." . . . "Take thou authority to preach the Word of God, and to minister the Holy Sacraments."[31]

Though Moberly finds the supreme expression of ministerial priesthood in the celebration of sacraments and especially in the liturgical

31. Ibid., 287–288.

leadership of the Eucharist, he is no mere ceremonialist. He defends the Anglican Ordinal for having a proper understanding of the relationship of liturgical leadership and sacramental ministry to the teaching and ruling dimension of the pastoral office.

> But I do say that he who finds the whole meaning of his priesthood in the act of celebrating does not at all understand what Christian priesthood truly means; and that if any Church should teach that Christian priesthood simply meant this, she would teach the meaning of priesthood definitely amiss. The "inwardness" of a true priesthood requires the dedication of the inner life to Godward; of which again a necessary aspect or corollary is dedication of self on behalf of "the others"—interceding for them, thinking for them, living for them, enduring for them. It is not that this "for other-ness" will always take the same form. Plainly the priest who is permanently invalided may illustrate perfectly the priestly spirit in his intercession for his brethren, which is perhaps the directest correlative of his right to present before them their ceremonial "offering." It may be in preaching, or in writing; in counselling or teaching; in organizing or visiting; or just in maintaining an integrity, and, in love, suffering for doing so; in any average parochial sphere it will probably be in some measure of every one of these things: but however opportunities and conditions may differ, some correlative measure there must be of the utterance of that inwardness which is as the breath of every priesthood that is not self-condemned as merely official and formal; and which, however indirectly, is itself already an illustration of the meaning of pastoral love. I do not think it is anything like a fanciful analogy to say that the perfect outward and the perfect inward, the ideal pastorate and ideal priesthood, are blended together as one indivisible reality in the words of St. John, ch. X, "I am the good shepherd: the good shepherd layeth down his life for the sheep."[32]

Moberly set forth a vision of the ministerial priesthood which was not narrowly ceremonial or ultramontane in the Roman Catholic sense. He took seriously the Reformation objections to priestly and sacrificial language applied to the ordained ministry because of the distortions associated with the pre-Reformation doctrines of the Mass. He defended both the Anglican reformers' reservations about and retention of this sacerdotal vocabulary. Moberly set forth ably the interdependence of a proper understanding of the priesthood of Christ and the priesthood of both the

---

32. Ibid., 293–294.

body of Christ and the ordained ministers of the body. He articulated an inspiring vision of the necessary connection between the outer functions of the ordained ministry and the inner spirit which is necessary to give those functions authentic expression. Moberly's exegesis of the biblical terms of sacrifice and priesthood stands up very well to contemporary scholarship. His exposition of the ministerial priesthood not as over against the church but in and for the church would be at home in a contemporary ecumenical discussion of ordained ministry.[33] I have let Moberly speak at length in his own words because the words are so very good and so shot through with the priestly spirit of love and sacrifice with which he sought to inspire the ordained ministers of his day.

Are Anglican presbyters priests? I believe they are, and I believe that this assertion can be made in the face of accusations that an emphasis on the priesthood of the ordained ministry runs the risk of undermining the doctrines of justification by grace and the priesthood of all believers. Among other things, Moberly has persuasively shown that a neglect of the priestly character of the ordained ministry inevitably will result in a loss of priestly consciousness in the whole people of God. I believe Anglican presbyters and bishops are appropriately called priests because I have come to understand the ministerial priesthood of the ordained in the way R.C. Moberly so ably set out in this true Anglican classic.

---

33. See for instance the elucidation of the Anglican/ Roman Catholic International Commission statement on ministry. "Here the ordained ministry is firmly placed in the context of the ministry of the whole Church and exists for the service of all the faithful." ARCIC, "Doctrine of the Ministry."

3

Priesthood and Revelation

Toward the end of her life my mother was hospitalized. I was very fortunate that she was in a hospital that was between the rectory and the church and I was able to visit her easily. During the last few days she was unable to speak but our visits were still full of communication. After one such visit as I left with a very full heart, I noticed the newly opened hospital chapel. I went in with expectation, hope, and longing, and I was stunned, dazed by what I found. The room was beautiful and tasteful. There was fine woodwork, a soothing carpet, hushed lighting, and an abstract pattern that resembled clouds on the walls. It was an interfaith chapel and in the effort to be inclusive all specific content had been excluded. There were no explicit religious symbols of any kind, not Jewish, not Christian, not Buddhist. Even in the moment I understood the necessity and appropriateness of the choice but it did not keep me from feeling bereft. As I sat there with my heart full of thanksgiving and regret and a deep desire both to forgive and be forgiven, it is hard to imagine anything less satisfying than the abstract clouds floating in cones of artfully directed light. At that moment I would have given anything to see a crucifix with its assurance that God knows and redeems suffering, or a Christus Rex, with its proclamation of the Risen Christ reigning from the cross; a simple empty wooden cross, proclaiming both realities at once, would have been a great consolation.

I tried to think of what could be in a place like this. While I know that our public institutions now need to be sensitive to religions outside the Jewish-Christian traditions, somehow I felt that night if I could come up with something from Judaism that could be shared there might be some hope of the emptiness being filled. Of course, Judaism frowns on images.

To Persevere in Love

Then I thought of the Ten Commandments which you sometimes see written on the walls of churches. The Torah, The Way, The Ten Words. And then I thought of something which I had seen but not until that moment really understood. The image came to me of Torah processions. In synagogues it is the practice for the rabbi to take the scrolls of the Torah, which are vested and ornamented, in procession. The people reach out and touch the scrolls with great reverence and devotion, as if reaching out for life itself. Often this is a very solemn and decorous procession. But I had once seen a film of a Torah procession in a Hasidic community. A wild-eyed rabbi with long, curly sideburns and a black suit in disarray, with fringe peeking out of it, danced about fervently until the whole congregation was literally jumping for joy. And I understood: God speaks. In the emptiness, in the loneliness, to the fullness which cannot contain itself, God speaks. God does not leave us bereft but speaks and gives us a word, a word of love, a word of direction, a word of promise. God is not silent. God speaks. What joy, what inexpressible joy. What can one do save jump up and sing and fall down and pray? And what if this Word becomes flesh, as real and knowable as another person? What response could possibly be adequate to such a reality? First we should want to receive to the fullest extent possible this word, we would wish to reach out and touch it as if touching life itself and in so doing express our relief, gratitude and joy. We would want to offer praise and adoration that included conforming our lives to this word. Then would we not want to tell those who have not heard, have not seen, "That which was from the beginning, which we have heard, which we have seen with our eyes, which we have looked upon, and our hands have handled, of the Word of life" (1 John 1:1)? Would we not want to do this even at great cost, even if the price were high? Here is a first clue to the life of the priest, whether that priesthood of which every member of the church shares or the special calling of the ordained, that priesthood has to do with revelation, with the God who speaks and with responding to the word which is spoken with relief, gratitude, joy, obedience, and with costly, sacrificial witness. The priest is one who is a living testimony that God speaks and addresses humankind with a welcome word of love, direction and promise.

There has always been a choice between those religions that believe in revelation, in a God who speaks, and those that do not. Judaism, Christianity, and Islam on the one side, and something like Zen, which is completely agnostic about God or the gods, on the other. There has always been a choice between versions of revealed religion. There has always been the choice to believe or reject the Word spoken to us in Jesus Christ. Is this

Priesthood and Revelation

word a dependable word or no? It is of the nature of revelation that it is to be accepted or rejected. There is the inescapable choice, God speaks or not, this is God's word or not. What is unique in our own time is the attack on revelation in the heart of the church. This fundamental choice between a trust in God's word and a distrust is part of the theological discussion at the center of the church today. I do not mean to call into question the undoubted usefulness of exegetical tools and biblical scholarship which are of help in sharpening and refining our interpretation. But there is a feeling, which has arisen perhaps because of an overconfidence in and misuse of historical-critical methods, that the Bible is primarily a cultural artifact with very limited relevance and that Jesus Christ is perhaps one of the words which God may have spoken alongside many other words to which we also must listen. One of the giants of twentieth century theology Emil Brunner was asked about this problem of the dependability of revelation, and he answered that though there is wisdom and beauty in the world's great religions, there you will never hear the voice of the Good Shepherd calling his sheep by name. The priest is one who has heard a voice, the voice of the Good Shepherd calling the sheep by name, and who with rapture and with rapt attention says "listen, listen, do you hear that." It is the singularity, the uniqueness of revelation that produces a priest, this obsessive witness to the word from beyond with which God addresses our longing and hope. The priest is a person who wagers everything on the conviction that God speaks and that the voice of God can be heard, and God help us because it is such an audacious claim, that it is possible to be a servant of this voice and help others to hear this word of love, of direction, of promise as though it was directed directly to them because in fact it is directed directly to each and every one, everyone, everywhere. This is the sort of person you send for when you are facing death, your own or of those you love. When you are facing death, you want to know someone who is confident that there is a God and that God cares and that God can be known. You want someone utterly consecrated to that reality. You want a priest.

Much is made today of the reality of the mystery of God. God is inherently mysterious, it is said. It is said that all we say about God is metaphorical and analogical. It is said that all we say about God is therefore thought to be limited, tentative, provisional. Very often wise things are said about St. Gregory Nanzianan and the apophatic Greek tradition. It is claimed that it is really very ancient Patristic Theology that God is primarily and fundamentally ineffable mystery. Therefore we must be very humble in what we say and not claim too much. We must listen attentively to other claims and perhaps by collecting enough metaphors from enough traditions we will have our little theological worlds expanded and arrive at a greater approximation of the truth which we are instructed is an ideal term which perpetually recedes as we approach. Apparently by combining one undependable tradition with another undependable tradition and assessing the combination on the basis of some undisclosed and unaccountably dependable principle we come to truth by adding up falsehoods.

Of course there are limits to what we say about God; these limits are well known in the history of theology. But when the Fathers of the Church pointed to the mystery of God they wanted to point to the superabundance of meaning in God, not to empty the word God of all meaning. St. Gregory had no doubt that Jesus Christ was the one word of God addressed to humanity and that this word was a word of personal, sacrificial love. The great thing that Christianity brought to the ancient world was certainty, revelation, dependable knowledge about God. The ancient world was weary of comparative religion and philosophical speculation. Confusion and uncertainty had cut the moral nerve of the society and left the individual aimless, prone to ennui and jaded by the diminishing effectiveness of distractions like the games. It was the appearance of those first priests with their certainty that both attracted and repelled the ancient world. It was the appearance of certainty in the midst of uncertainty, of conviction in the midst of confusion. In a world in which people were not sure who the gods might be, there appeared a group of people who were so certain that they had heard God, had met God, that they were willing to die for God and who dying proclaimed the possibility for their persecutors to hear and know God also, even to be forgiven for the crime of persecuting God's messenger. It was this priestly, sacrificial life on the part of the Apostles and the ordinary Christians who heeded them that created the early church. Of course we must have humility and restraint, and say no more than has been given to us. What has been given to us is the life of Jesus Christ, a life lived with utter conviction in the reality of his Father and the Father's will that we should repent and return and heed the word of love and forgiveness directed to us in His Son.

Jesus Christ perseveres in love, perseveres in bringing us God's Word, perseveres in being God's Word, perseveres to the end, perseveres in the face of great hostility, perseveres to the Cross and thereby opens the way to eternal life, a new life that begins now and which the grave cannot hold. It is this perseverance in love, based on confidence in the Father and certainty about His love and purpose, which produces the sacrificial, priestly life of

Priesthood and Revelation

Jesus Christ and which has the power to bring us to redemption, to the place where we can hear and obey. The listening, hearing, obeying of the Son produces the priesthood of Christ and of His Body the Church. Within the church there are those whose ministry it is to continually reconstitute the church by virtue of their utter consecration to the reality of God's Word. It is the sacramental priesthood of the church's ordained ministers that makes possible a fresh hearing of the Word of God and animates the life of believers with the conviction that leads to praise, adoration and sacrifice, to the priesthood of all believers. The figure of the ordained, sacramental priest disappears when confidence in Jesus Christ as the one Word of God disappears, for Christ's own priesthood is disappearing and with the loss of this confidence on the part of the ordained ministers, the whole priestly life of the church in all its members begins to dissipate. In the place of relief, gratitude, joy, adoration, praise and self-offering (sacrifice is grateful self-offering), there begins to creep in a spirit of striving and pride. With striving and pride come their twins, exhaustion and despair. If there is no dependable revelation, then we are condemned to an exhausting search. If there is no definitive gift of salvation in the sacrificial life of Christ, then we must try and must fail to reach God ourselves and in some way fabricate our own salvation out of good works or spirituality. We should expect that when confidence in the one Word of persevering love that comes to us in Jesus Christ begins to be lost there should come into the life of the church and its ministers a restless, frenetic quality, a seeking without finding, a striving that leads to disappointment and despair.

The church lives from the grateful, joyous, free self-offering of the Son to the Father in the power of the Spirit. The inner life of the Trinity is a life of praise, adoration, and joyous self-offering. The inner life of the Trinity is a priestly life, a going out in persevering love, a return in loving praise and sacrifice. It is the mission of the Son to bring this priestly life, this sacrificial persevering love to light, and so He comes in the power of the life He has with the Father, in the power of the Spirit, to be the light and life of the world, to be the one Word of divine persevering love. Yet, He cannot really bring us this love without persevering to the end with a listening, an obedience that extends even to the cross. Only when rebellion, resistance, and hatred have been drowned in the blood (the sacrificial love) of the cross, only when the tide of hate and rebellion flowing from the evil one has been overwhelmed by the tide of love flowing from the Father and pouring out through the wounded side of Christ, only then through that total self-offering, does the new life of the Resurrection appear and it becomes possible for sacrificial, persevering love to do its recreating work. Had the Risen Christ no wounds in His hands, His feet, His side, He could not quicken us. It is the love that perseveres unto the death of the cross that is His peace, which He breathes into the Apostles that first Easter. It is a peace that the world cannot give. It comes from above and it is bought at great price.

This peace, this joy, this sacrifice, cannot come to us abstractly, cannot come as a theory, an idea. It must come as He came: in a particular time, in a particular place, in a particular person. It must come by one who has heard this word, "As the Father has sent me, even so I send you" (John 20:21). And I dare to add, for it is said in so many words, Persevere in love as I have persevered. Die with me so that you may live and so that by the witness of your dying and rising others may be brought to life, and that which I said to you in the beginning, by the side of the lake will surely come true, Follow me and you shall catch people alive.

It will instantly be said that this is the duty of all Christians, and so it is. The life that Jesus Christ lived was the duty of every human being, but the Father had to send the Son to persevere in love, to make this life a possibility for us. So the Son provides for an effective sign of His persevering love in the midst of His people. So a particular person in a particular time, in a particular place, is ordained, consecrated, set apart to make present the death of Christ which is our life, to by a priestly life of praise, adoration, and grateful sacrifice, call others to the death by which they may live and find the life for which they were made as members of the Body of Christ, as a Royal Nation, as a Kingdom of Priests.

But how is it possible to have this confidence? Is this something that a modern, an enlightened, person can really do? Do we not know too much to so completely trust one claim and only one among so many claims to be the definitive word of God? Does not anyone who claims such confidence risk being a hypocrite who suppresses honest doubt? These are legitimate questions and they must be addressed. But we must see what is at stake. At stake is the life of faith itself, especially in its priestly dimension as a life of commitment, consecration, and sacrifice, a complete trust. A commitment with a reserve held back for the truth which might yet appear cannot qualify as a priestly service of praise and self-offering.

There are two parts to this question. In part, this is a philosophical and theological question. It is a matter of foundational choices about first principles. To assume that there can in principle be no one trustworthy Word

Priesthood and Revelation

of God is a foundational choice, a faith in itself, an ultimate commitment which can be justified on the basis of no other more ultimate principle. It is a choice and commitment of the same nature and structure as the choice to believe in a God who speaks, who reveals himself in a gracious word of persevering sacrificial love. It is not inherently more rational, more plausible, to disbelieve in a definitive revelation. The conviction that such faith is overreaching or lacking in intellectual integrity comes from an uncritical, excessive trust in the illusion of a disinterested, critical principle. So in part the charge of a faith that overreaches needs to be met by the unmasking of an overreaching, critical-rationalism. Martin Luther once called reason a whore by which he meant that it is all too easy to rationalize our denial of God. The introduction into the heart of the church of a distrust in revelation as a first principle more basic and dependable than a fundamental trust in the goodness of God and effective desire of God to be known is precisely the sort of thing of which Luther was speaking, and which must be condemned as a false intellectualism and a kind of anti-theology.

Once it is established that the conviction that revelation is undependable is not inherently more intellectually respectable than the conviction that there is one dependable Word of God, there remains another part of the problem—the problem of the human heart which both yearns to give itself totally and completely and which yet draws back at the moment of commitment. We can have hesitations that are not only intellectual, but that have to do with the fear of vulnerability that comes from such total commitment. Even if I can come to a moment of clarity, conviction and commitment, it is hard to sustain, and soon I am assailed by doubts which no strength of argument can suppress. Once we acknowledge that the one Word of God addressed to us in Jesus Christ cannot be said in principle to be untrustworthy, how do we bring ourselves in actual fact to trust and commitment? How do we silence the voices within and without, which tell us to go slow, be cautious, hedge our bets, and to protect ourselves by refraining from the kind of total commitment that can lead to a terrible exposure, to an insupportable vulnerability?

The call to Christian Faith, to bet your life on Jesus Christ, is not a call to silence all those interior or exterior voices. It is not a call to be completely sure and confident before commitment. It is a call to die, to bet everything, holding nothing back. We want all questions to be settled first and then we will commit ourselves. We will always have doubts, fears, voices within and without that will give us pause, that will hold us back. There will never be an end to this kind of hesitation. The order is not first the elimination of doubt, and then commitment, faith, the life of obedience and sacrifice, the priestly life. The order is trust, commitment, sacrifice, the priestly life, and from this comes the growing conviction of the faithfulness of God which draws forth praise and adoration. In this growing life of faith, doubts and hesitations can have a dynamic role and lead to greater assurance and conviction. As the priestly life of sacrifice and praise is pursued in the face of doubts and fears, and God is again and again found faithful to save, as the profound dependability of the Word of persevering love that has come in the flesh of Jesus Christ becomes more evident, the adoration, praise, and sacrifice, the consecration of the priest grows, and so does the effectiveness of this sacramental presence of Christ in His church.

It is appropriate, it is necessary, it is indispensable to the life of faith and especially to that life as a priestly life of praise and sacrifice that solemn and in principle irrevocable commitments should be made in spite of doubts and fears, with the realistic expectation that doubts and fears will never completely disappear, that they even have a providential role in God's plan of salvation. But it is not doubts and fears that are meant by God to determine the shape of human life but unswerving commitment to the One Word of God's persevering love addressed to us in Jesus Christ. So the promise to trust Christ and follow Him as Lord and Savior that is made in Baptism is regarded as an irrevocable commitment. It cannot be allowed that the mistrust of this commitment can lead to the life for which we were made. There are no fears or doubts that can release us from our moment of commitment. The nature of the commitment is that it is to be maintained in the face of doubts and fears. The promise is that in this struggle, faith and character will grow.

Over and over again in the life of the church, Christian people are asked to deepen their commitments to Christ and each other in the face of and in spite of fears and doubts. Those who have been baptized at an early age are asked to renew their covenant in Confirmation. A man and a woman are asked to bring alive in a unique way Christ's irrevocable commitment to us, by making an irrevocable commitment to each other. We are asked Sunday by Sunday to renew, reaffirm our faith. These requests come with an understanding and acknowledgment of the doubts and fears that assail us. The teaching office of the Church subverts itself when it speaks without seeming to have knowledge of or sympathy for these very real doubts and fears. Nevertheless, it is the reaffirmation of faith that gives the gift of a life of praise, thanksgiving, and sacrifice. It is the renewal of faith in the face of doubt that arises in a suffering and sinful world that is meant by God to structure our lives, and give life and hope. In the midst of the necessity, the demand, and the difficulty of renewing faith and making an irrevocable commitment, the commitment of the sacrificial, sacramental priest has a special role. The invitation of Jesus Christ to follow Him in complete trust, complete dependence, total self-giving to the Father, comes to the life of the faithful, gathered together in a congregation, not as an abstract principle, not as a theory but through a unique person who embodies a unique irreplaceable and irrevocable commitment to Jesus Christ and to his Church. It is vital, indispensable, and uniquely constitutive of the sacramental priesthood that the priest makes an irrevocable and life-long commitment to the service of Christ's Church in Word and Sacrament. Such a commitment is made not by silencing voices within and without that protest the extravagance of such a vow, but in spite of them, and with the determination that faith and not doubt shall determine the shape of this life. "As for me and my house we shall serve the Lord" (Josh 24:15). The priest makes ordination vows knowing many doubts and fears and knowing that many more will come. Moments of deepening faith will bring a deepening crisis of doubt and trust. It is the reckless and wild abandonment of such a commitment that Christ uses to keep alive at the heart of the church His own recklessness in love and wild abandonment to the will of His Father. The grace of ordination works in and through the commitment of the priest, the abandonment of the priest to the priestly life, to elicit commitment and sacrifice in the people despite their doubts and fears.

One thing that gives many people pause when they contemplate the vocation of Holy Orders is the obvious dependence of the parish priest on the life of the congregation. It is perceived and rightly so, that the priest is at the mercy of the congregation, that failure and rejection in this role can be devastating in way that threatens to overwhelm, and from which recovery is hard to imagine. Sometimes this reality keeps people from the priesthood. Sometimes ordinands try to minimize the effect by choosing specialized ministries like teaching, chaplaincy, or pastoral counseling. Such efforts are ineffective. This dependence and vulnerability are inherent in the priesthood because they are inherent in the priesthood of Jesus Christ. He makes Himself uniquely and irrevocably dependent on us. He makes Himself vulnerable to being rejected by his own. His passion—the suffering of the cross—is the suffering of one rejected by His own. It is not possible to embrace the life of the priest without embracing the cross, this death by which He gives life, and the cross will be there all the same in the classroom, the hospital, and the counseling session. The priest will be there with this vulnerability that comes from complete abandonment to the one Word of God's persevering love and with the necessity to persevere in the face of rejection and hostility. Vulnerability is part of the sacramental witness of the priesthood to the priestly life of Christ in our midst as He calls us all to risk all with Him for the sake of His Father and His Father's children. The endurance of hostility and rejection are part of the life of every priest and part of the life of the priestly people of God. For most parish priests most of the time this is balanced by the real love of the people for the faithful priest. Many priests have experienced at some time a very complete rejection by the people to which they have committed themselves. Such a rejection is perhaps not inevitable but it is a likely experience at some point in the priestly life given both the frailty of priest and people. But even in such a moment there is not a failure of the sacramental sign which Christ gives to the church in the sacramental priesthood. Even in failure and rejection, even when removed from office because of relational incompetence or popular demand, the vulnerability of the priest to the loyalty of the people brings to light the way in which Christ puts himself at the disposal of His people and the way in which the redeeming presence is at work in our midst, suffering our indifference and rejection.

Less and less do I feel that effectiveness in the exercise of the sacramental priesthood has to do with skill and competence; more and more I feel that effectiveness has to do with surrender, abandonment, dependence, and vulnerability. This should not be confused with an imprudent disregard for developing skills and competencies appropriate to one's office. We are duty bound to be diligent and disciplined. We must try to infuse our relationships with our fellows with warmth and Christian affection. But these things only grant the occasion, the opportunity, for the grace of ordination to work and that grace is dependent on the living response to a Word that is revealed. The grace of ordination depends on surrender to the costly, sacrificial, persevering Word of God's love by abandonment to that Word in the care of God's people. It is the willingness to die with Christ that we might rise with Him that is at the root of the priesthood of both the sacramental priest and the priestly people. It is trust in His Word that if we would find our lives we must lose them.

4

The Priesthood and Glory

GLORY, KABOD IN HEBREW, *doxa* in Greek, is one of the most important words in all of scripture. The lexicons tell us that the word has to do with weight, heft, and also with shimmering light. The word has the sense of power and majesty, and even danger and threat. When the lookout put his hand over his forehead and searched the horizon and there saw the shimmering reflection of the desert sun on the spear points and chariot wheels of an approaching army, he would say that he had seen the glory of an army. If it were an enemy army, it meant threat and danger; if it were an ally, it meant rescue and salvation. When the people of Israel were encamped before the Red Sea, the lookouts sounded the alarm, "Behold, here comes Pharaoh and all his glory." Moses stretched out his hand and said, "Behold, the glory of the Lord" (Exod 14).

There is the closest association between the glory of the Lord and the salvation of the Lord in the scriptures. Moses, the Prince of Egypt, is raised in the midst of the glory of Pharaoh. The secret of his birth as a Hebrew slave emerges in his life and he becomes a murderer and an exile. He falls from the glorious life of an Egyptian noble to the humble life of a shepherd. To one who has lost his glory there appears the glory of the Lord in the vision of the burning bush. So Moses turns aside to see this sight, this bush that burns and is not consumed, and there he encounters the glory of the Lord. He is overcome with wonder and awe at the presence of the God of glory. He hides his face because he was afraid to look upon the glory of the Lord. Here, out of His glory, God speaks to Moses and calls him to be an agent of God's answer to the cries of God's people, and to take a role in God's plan of salvation. It is inconceivable that Moses could persist in his vocation, his calling to bring a message of redemption to Israel, to bring a message of judgment to Egypt, without this vision of the glory of the Lord which he sees and yet dares not look upon. Moses has to persist in the face of the unbelief of both the house of Jacob and the house of Pharaoh. Moses has to persist in bringing the promise of redemption which has hidden within it a word of judgment and a call to repentance. Moses has to persist in bringing a promise of judgment which has hidden within it a word of forgiveness and grace. God has allowed Moses to draw near and to perceive God's glory so that God can use Moses to forward the plan of salvation.

In this calling of Moses there appears a fundamental aspect of the priestly life. It is a life that is a witness to the glory of the Lord. The priest is someone who has seen something which is beautiful, fearsome, and precisely awe-full. The priest is someone who has seen something that one longs to see, that one turns aside to see, for which one lays aside the ordinary business of life so that one may see, and yet this something, this vision of the glory of God is something from which, at the first real glimpse of it, we draw back and hide our eyes, because we are afraid to look. But the priest has seen enough to know what it is to be afraid to look upon the glory of God, to be caught between the irresistible attraction of that terrible beauty and the fear that one will be incinerated, consumed. The priest has seen something that cannot be seen and this sight changes everything. There is really no possibility of a return to ordinary business, ordinary life. To see this thing which cannot be seen, to become in this way aware of the glory of God, means to be confronted with the demand of God in an irresistible way. The thicket of ordinary life in which we hide from God is burned away in that moment of vision and there is left only this bush which burns but is not consumed. In the light of that fire there is no longer a place to hide from God's call to be an instrument of God's plan of salvation. I do not think there is in the Scriptures a record of the vision of the glory of God which is not also part of a command and demand by God to become a herald, an instrument, in God's plan of salvation. So God says to Moses, "Go tell old Pharaoh, Let my people go"(Exod 3:10). Moses goes with this indefatigable conviction about the glory of the Lord. He is able to persist in his testimony to God's will to redeem His people. He is able to persist in speaking a word of hope to those who disbelieve because of despair, and he is able to persist in speaking a word of warning to those who disbelieve because of an exaggerated self-confidence. Moses demands the impossible from both the slave and the king. He persists in these improbable demands at great cost, at the

The Priesthood and Glory

risk of being thought mad or a fool or a charlatan. Moses persists in giving a testimony to God's glorious plan of salvation to people who have not seen the glory of the Lord and who in the present moment because of despair or hardness of heart cannot see, but Moses has seen, and seen enough so that he cannot pretend that he has not seen. He must continue and persist in his life of worshipping witness and sacrificial service to the vision of glory that the Lord has granted him, to the vocation of message bearer to which this vision commits him. All the while he desires with all his soul to see more and fears the destruction that he knows must come with a fuller vision.

This gift to Moses of a vision of the glory of God is the means by which God calls Moses to his vocation to be a messenger of salvation. It is the means by which God strengthens Moses for the contemptuous and disbelieving reception Moses is bound to encounter from both Hebrew and Egyptian. The purpose of this vision granted to an individual is not to set up some spiritual elite with a monopoly on the vision of the Lord. Indeed, we know that Moses is no clericalist in this sense but that he hopes "that all the Lord's people might be prophets" (Num 11:29). The purpose is to lead Hebrew and Egyptian alike to perceive the greatness of God and the glory of the Lord. It is the way God works that He calls the many by calling an individual to be a minister, a servant, a priest. The vision of glory granted to Moses consecrates him, sets him apart for a life of witness, worship, and sacrifice, makes him a herald of salvation and a priest. The gift of the vision of God's glory which Moses treasures in his heart makes it possible for him to persist in his vocation of preparing people to see and respond to the glory of the Lord. The Hebrew people are able to answer the call to leave their slavery and go quickly because they have been made ready by the witness of Moses. They are led out not by Moses but by the glory itself, which appears to them in form of a cloud by day and a pillar of fire by night.

There is a relationship between Moses' own desire to come closer to the glory of the Lord and the growing relationship between God and the people. They come to that mountain and there is fire and smoke on the mountain. The glory of the Lord is there and the people are afraid. We may not doubt that Moses is afraid. Moses has seen enough that he wants to see more. He has seen enough that he knows that his calling is to draw closer, not only for himself to satisfy his own spiritual curiosity, but for the sake of these people. It is inherent in the priestly life that the pursuit of the vision of the glory of God is something that has always more than personal consequences. In the response to the call of God, in the response to the vision of God's glory, in the quest for a fuller vision of that glory, there is always at work this desire of God to reach others, to touch other lives and draw them closer. The spirituality of the priest is inherently public. It is not for nothing in the Anglican tradition that the priest is called the parson, the public person. This drama of Moses and the mountain, shall he go higher, shall he go up to meet the face of the Lord, shall he come back with some word of the Lord, is reported with great interest. If here Moses loses courage, if he refuses to make the climb, then God's desire to bring a word to God's people is thwarted and God must find another way. People instinctively resent the priest who has drawn back and refuses to go farther and who has thus betrayed the priestly vocation. People inherently resent a church that draws back and refuses to go farther and thus has betrayed the call to be a priestly people. Sometimes, though there is an inner resentment of this loss of courage and lack of nerve, there can be an outward acceptance and even colluding encouragement in superficiality because people rightly fear the glory of the Lord, and both hope and fear that the priest will seek the face of God. It is a great blessing when a priest of the church serves among people who encourage the priest to go higher, to draw closer.

The vision of that bush burning within his heart propels Moses up the mountain in spite of his intuition that, unlike the bush, he might burn and be consumed. Upon the mountain Moses is entrusted with the Torah, with the Word of God's law. This is part of the gift of glory that God wants to give to the people. The glory of God that dawned the first day of creation and that called to Moses out of the burning bush is in those ten words, in that revelation of God's law. The Ten Commandments are resplendent with the holiness, righteousness, and the majesty of God. In the Torah we see that the goodness of God and the glory of God are one. God is awesome, powerful and just, and righteous. God reveals His glory by calling the people to goodness and righteousness, and shows God's own goodness by showing the people how to live toward God and how to live toward one another. God had sent them a messenger to call them from the slavery of Egypt to freedom. Now through that same messenger God calls them from the slavery of sin and evil to the free life of worship, sacrifice, and service. God sends them a priest who calls them to a priestly life. God redeems a man from exile and saves him so that through him God might make plain the path of salvation to God's people. In all of this, God is revealing God's glory. God is revealing power, might, majesty, light. The structure of this revelation is first to the one and through the one to the many. It is a pattern that will be repeated again and again and will find a consummation in the ministry of Jesus, and which Jesus will reconstitute in His own way as he calls this one and that one so that many may come from East and West, North and South, to eat at table in the Kingdom. The call to live in the light of the glory of God comes through the person who has been drawn into the priestly life through witnessing the glory of God. This initial witness came to Moses through the burning bush. It was confirmed by the miracles of Egypt and the mystery of the Passover, in the revelation of the Ten Words upon the mountain. It continued to be witnessed to and ministered to the people as a living presence in the ministry of Tabernacle and Temple. The weight of this glory was felt as an aching absence when the priests and people turned away from God and toward the idols. This is the glory that descended upon Jesus like a dove at His Baptism, that is revealed in His life of teaching and healing, redeeming and absolving, as He restores the lost sheep of Israel. His life was a life attended by signs and wonders in power and glory. This glory is above all seen in that persistence of love in the face of sin and evil which is the cross of Jesus Christ. This glory is the same glory of the risen and ascended Lord, and the same glory which is gifted to the church through the Spirit. This glory reveals itself as more than raw power, as not only majesty but goodness, in these words of love that call the people to salvation, that call them to a way of life that is life lived in light of the glory of God, to a way of life that reflects the glory of God.

The path to ordination in the church often begins with a glimpse of the burning bush. For me there were two places where as a child I encountered the vision of the glory of God. One was in nature, in the created order. There was a place where I used to go in the woods when I was a small child of five or so that was full of light and that also spoke to me of an awesome, even fearsome power, that was fearsome not because it was bad but good, that was threatening not because it was bad but good. I both feared and loved to go to that place. Later when I came to the sacraments of the church, I saw that this same glory was in the church and at the heart of its worship. As a child, I saw that the altar where the Eucharist was celebrated held that same light, that same glory that I had witnessed in that clearing in the woods. Later I began to hear that glory, that majesty, that immense and fearsome goodness in the words of the Bible. The priest is one who is a witness to the glory of the Lord in creation, in the mighty deeds of God as He delivers the captives and in the words of God's Word. Moses is the pre-eminent priest of the Old Testament. He is the one called to bear the Word of God to God's disbelieving people and to a hostile world. He is completely consecrated to this task, and this calling, this ordination, this anointing by God marks him, changes him. His hair turns white, his face glows with the reflected glory of the encounter with God. The people find the sight of the reflected glory so frightening that he has to veil his face when he talks with them. (The traditional theology of priesthood as an indelible character is not elitist speculation. It is an attempt to put into the precise language of theology the most commonplace of observations that a life set apart for the service of God's Word leaves a mark.)

What did the people see when they saw Moses with the veil upon his face? They saw someone who by his very person, by his being, was a witness to the glory of the Lord and to the awesome authority of the Word of God. Through Moses, God draws the people to Himself and evokes in them awe, reverence, and an attentive listening to God's Word. When they see the veil and the radiance upon Moses' face, they know they look upon the prophet of the Lord who bears the Word of God. They know that they look upon the priest of God, the consecrated mediator between God and His people. The personality of Moses recedes. It does not disappear. He is still a man, and in the moments when the radiance is not upon him and the veil is not upon his face, they have no trouble recognizing him as such. One moment they are in awe of him, and the next moment they treat him with contempt and disrespect. But when he first comes down from the mountain having been allowed only to glimpse the glory of the Lord going by, and subsequently when he emerges from the Tabernacle when the shekinah glory is upon the tent in a cloud, his veiled face shining from the encounter, his personality does not disappear but recedes into the background and it is his ministry that is in the foreground. When the radiance is upon him they do not see Moses, the man, so much as Moses, the bearer of God's Word, the witness of God's glory, God's representative to them, their intercessor with God. When Moses appears before the people of God, his face veiled and radiant with the reflected glory of God, he is completely identifiable as the priest of the most high God, as the one through whom God makes his terrible yet tender appeal to His people. In the fullness of time, God himself will take the veil, and the glory, veiled in humanity and by the mystery of the cross, will draw His people unimaginably close to His awesome glory, and bring them to the place where they can go boldly behind the veil, and come themselves to stand even closer to God than Moses did upon the mountain: "and behold the veil of the Temple was torn in two" (Luke 23:45).

The Priesthood and Glory

The Christian priest, the priest of the new Israel is the witness of and servant of the glory, the glory of the cross and resurrection of Jesus Christ. "No one has ever seen the Father (not even Moses from whom God held back a complete revelation of His glory lest he die) but we have seen His glory, glory as of the only begotten Son of the Father, in the face of Jesus Christ" (John 1:14,18). When the priest appears at the Eucharist in radiant vesture, there is a veil upon the face of the priest and the personality of the priest recedes. It does not disappear. It cannot. It should not, but it recedes and we remember the words of John the Baptist, "I must decrease, that He may increase" (John 3:30). And the words of St. Paul, "Not I, but Christ liveth in me" (Gal 2:20), and "I carry about in myself the marks of the death of Christ that the life of Christ might be made known as well" (2 Cor 4:10). As the priest appears in the holy vestments, veiled for the service of God and the service of God's people, the people see the one who has been set apart by God to be His witness to His glory, to be the messenger of His Word, and to be the intercessor and the go-between. The priest vested at the Eucharist is veiled that the people might see the glory of the Lord in the life and death and resurrection of the Messiah, and that they might be taken up in that glory as they "lift up their hearts" and join the song of the angels and archangels who behold the glory of heaven. So the Christian priest, so to speak, dons the veil of Moses and the people see not the glory reflected in the face of Moses but the glory of God in the face of Jesus Christ as He takes the bread and says, "this is my body broken for you," and takes the cup and says, "this is my blood of the New Covenant." "Take, eat, for my flesh is food indeed and my blood is drink indeed." And once again the veil of the Temple is torn from top to bottom and the tombs are opened and the dead are seen alive.

I have passed quickly from the veil upon the face of Moses, to the veiled divinity of the Incarnate Son by whose death and resurrection God is able to unveil His glory amongst us and bring us by, with, and in Christ to the glory of eternal life. I have not lingered on the wilderness Tabernacle or the Temple of Jerusalem with its holy of holies behind the veil. I have gone quickly to the removal of that veil and the long-awaited revealing of the glory of God in Jesus Christ. In the Tabernacle and the Temple, the veil upon the radiant face of Moses gives rise to two garments, the veil that separates the holy of holies and hides the overwhelming glory of the Lord upon the mercy seat, and the vestments of Aaron and his sons. These beautiful garments represent to the people the radiance upon the face of Moses.

They are witnesses to the glory of the Lord, and they allow the people to see God at work in and through His ministers making His people holy. The vested priests and the service of the Tabernacle make possible a continuing liturgical presence of the revelation of the Word of God in power and glory. The sacraments of Baptism and Eucharist perform the same function for the new Israel.

There is a recent tendency in the churches that have cherished the catholic priesthood for the clergy to abandon their distinctive dress in their day to day work and even to abandon all but the most simple and plain Eucharistic vestments. The reason given is a commendable desire to eschew "elitism" and "clericalism" and to avoid ostentation and show solidarity with the poor. In fact what happens is that the veil of Moses, which is the distinctive mark of the biblical priesthood of Moses and Aaron and more perfectly of Jesus Christ, is laid aside. Instead of the role of priest having preeminence and the personality of the priest its rightful but secondary place in the background, the personality and agenda of the person take the front ground and the center stage. We should not be surprised if it becomes difficult for the people to know when we are appearing not in our own right with our own word but with the radiance of the Lord upon us as we speak not our word but His. We should not be surprised if a reluctance to don the veil, which expresses itself in so many ways including such apparently indifferent things as the manner of dress, should not cause us who are priests to become confused ourselves between our understandable human agendas and our role as witnesses to a glory not our own, mediators of a life not our own, intercessors for a mercy not our own, as priests through whom the Father makes present His glory in the service of His Word and sacrament.

This service of Word and sacrament is a witness to the glory of God in the life, death, and resurrection of Jesus Christ, and of the gift of the ascended Lord's glorified life to His people in the power of the Spirit. The priest is a witness to the transfiguring power of the glorified Lord both to individual souls and to the gathered community. This witness is on the model of the witness of Aaron and his sons. It is not a witness to a past event but to a present, living reality whose glory is perceived and understood as the continuing presence of the God of glory who has acted decisively for the salvation of His people. The Tabernacle is a witness to the present active glory of the God who has definitively revealed Himself on Sinai. Moses dies. The original witnesses of Moses die but in the worship and ministry

The Priesthood and Glory

of the Old Testament, God has provided that His glory will never lack a witness consecrated to make present as a living reality the mighty deeds of God on behalf of His people, to recount to the people the words God spake to Moses as a living Word which calls out faith, worship, thanksgiving, and sacrificial obedience. Likewise, the witness of the Apostles is not a witness to an event which is past but to the decisive intervention of God into the life of the world in the life, death, and resurrection of the Lord, and to the continuing presence of the Risen Lord in the midst of the church as he redeems, saves and transfigures His people. The priest is a witness to the glory of God who speaks and acts to save His people. The liturgy, the energetic and energizing work of the priest and people (in the case of both the Old Testament and the New Testament itself given as a gift directly from the hands of God) is to make it possible for the people to reconstitute themselves as a saved company, as the people of God, in such a way that they come once again to Sinai and a reverent hearing of God's Word, come once again to the night in which He was betrayed and hear the words of the Word made flesh as He offers them His Life of worship and obedience, of sacrifice and service, which is to be poured out for them on the cross, which is to be raised victorious and that will pour forth by the power of the Spirit at Pentecost.

The priest offers this liturgy of witness to the glory of God, a witness that is an active representation of a living reality, of a hidden but ever present glory, most completely in the celebration of the Holy Eucharist. For here the whole history of the saving deeds of God comes to completion and fulfillment, as the sacramental priests of the church witness to and represent the living presence of the Great High Priest as He forgives and absolves His people and blesses them with the gift of His eternal life. Away from the Eucharist, the great act of thankful witness, the priest continues the work of absolution and blessing by bringing forward and making active outside the liturgy, the glory of God in forgiveness and blessing, and the glory of His people repentant, forgiven, and blessed with everlasting fellowship with God.

To persist in the priestly life, the ordained priest needs to be convicted and reconvicted with the reality of the glory of God in God's word. For the people to persist as a priestly people they need to be convicted and reconvicted with the reality of the glory of God in God's word. To be the messenger and witness of this glory is the vocation of God's priest. God sends Moses down the mountain consecrated in a new way to the service of God's word. The word of God is no longer only a word in the ear of Moses. The word is a text, a collection of words that must be cherished, communicated, learned, studied, and transmitted from one generation to the next. It is the ministry of Moses now to bring these words to the people in such a way that they perceive the glory of God, that they feel the weight of them and see the light in them. "Thy word is a lamp unto my feet, and a light unto my path" (Ps 119:105). But this ministry of the Word is precisely a priestly ministry. It is a sacrificial ministry which is effective only when it draws forth sacrifice from the people. It is a prophetic ministry of proclamation that fails in its mission if it does not elicit adoration and worship. This ministry of being the herald of God's Word cannot be done apart from liturgy. The proclamation of God's Word requires a consecration of the messenger and a consecration of the people. So in Exodus 24:8, Moses takes the blood of a bull and throws it both upon the people and upon the altar, and the reading of the Word becomes the most awe-full, solemn, and sacred event. In the most visceral way, the life and death struggle by which they have been redeemed by God, the preciousness of the new life, the debt and honor owed to God, and the peril of denying their God are evoked. All of this Moses literally throws in their face by the crudest and yet profound ritual.

As children of the Reformation and a somewhat anti-Semitic tradition of Biblical scholarship, we are prone to overdraw the distinction between the ministry of the priest and the prophet and to create an imaginary religion, which unlike the actual religion of the Bible imagines a Word that is delivered without a liturgy and without a priesthood. The attack of the prophets on the priesthood is not an attack on a superfluous office but upon one which does not fulfill its function, on a priesthood which has failed to lead people to perceive the glory of the Lord and the awesomeness of His word, on a priesthood which has domesticated God and robbed God of His glory. The priesthood is criticized by the prophets because it has abandoned its function of creating a holy, a consecrated, a priestly people, a nation of witnesses to the glory of the Lord.

In the Bible, God's Word, God's glory, the messenger who is the witness and herald of this glory, who is consecrated by this glory and thus the priest of the glory of the Lord, and the people who respond in praise and adoration, in sacrifice and service and are thus the priestly people of the Lord, witnesses to the glory of God by worship and obedience, these things are indissoluble parts of the one act of God by which He saves and redeems His people. The Word never appears apart from a liturgy of praise

The Priesthood and Glory

and sacrifice even if it is only the pouring forth of the messenger's own blood in witness. This perfect priesthood is indeed the form of the perfect prophecy of Jesus Christ and in the sacred liturgy of the cross the Word of God is perfectly proclaimed and the people see the glory of the Lord and are made holy by it.

The path to ordination will be different for different people. It is doubtful anyone would persist in that path without some vision of the glory of God. It might be in creation, or in the worship of the church or in some more private, inner vision, or in the love given by a parent or some other witness to the glory of God. To persist in the priestly life, the ordained minister cannot do without a profound experience of the presence of the glory of God in God's Word, in the Bible. The desire to witness to that glory will allow one to persist as a preacher and teacher. Just to the extent that glory is recognized in the words of the Bible, the priest will bring to the liturgy of the church, and especially to that liturgy that is shot through with the glory of the proclamation of His own death and resurrection on "the night in which He was betrayed," a witness of reverence and awe, which serve God's one act of redemption through which God glorifies His people.

To "rightly and duly administer the sacraments" must mean among other things that the priest by virtue of a posture of awe, wonder, reverence, and care communicates to the people that it is the same glory of the Lord that is there at the Red Sea and upon the mountain, that shines forth in all the law and the prophets, that descends upon the Tabernacle in the desert and the Temple in Jerusalem. It is the same glory that Isaiah saw, in the year king Uzziah died, when he heard the witness song of the angels, "Holy, Holy, Holy" (Isa 6). The glory that Ezekiel saw leave the Temple and that he saw on the banks of the river of exile like wheels of fire, "way up in the middle of the air"(Ezek 1), that is the same glory that the prophets foresaw in the coming of the messiah, the one anointed to restore the glory of the kingdom and the Temple, all the same glory that appears at last in completion and fulfillment in the face of Jesus Christ, the Word made flesh, whose one glory is in the cross and the resurrection, and by the Spirit given by the ascended Lord in His people who become His body and His glory in the world and a token of the glory to come. It is the one glory that is in the words of the Bible, in the sacrifice of praise and thanksgiving that is the Eucharist, and in the people repentant and restored to fellowship with God and each other. This is the ministry and the witness of the priest.

5

The Priesthood and Doctrine

IN MANY OF OUR churches there are more people in the basement attending Twelve Step meetings during the week than there are attending the worship of the church on Sunday. If you attend these meetings, you discern a feeling, a sense of things that is absent from many of our churches. People come to the Twelve Step meetings because they are in a life or death struggle with what they call "a crippling disease." Sometimes this disease is given a personality. It is referred to as a "canny disease." "You can't outsmart it." Hope lies in attending the meetings and sharing in the faith, hope and encouragement that is there. Hope lies in attending to a teaching, a doctrine, the Twelve Steps, which are a matter of life and death and the only practical means of salvation from certain, sure, and complete destruction. (The seriousness with which this teaching is taken is shown in the prohibition against the discussion of literature which is not "conference approved.") But if destruction apart from the "program" is sure, inevitable, and complete, with the "program" there is a confident promise of recovery, healing, and new life. Meetings regularly include testimonies by people who have been saved by following the Steps and returned to sobriety and sanity. The contrast between the old life and the new life is dramatic and affecting. Often people express their gratitude for the disease which propelled them on a search which has led to a far better life than they would have otherwise had.

This sense of a life and death struggle with a real and canny evil, of being in the grip of a dark power, of being unable to extricate oneself and of needing (what else can it be called?) salvation, this sense that is so palpably present in these groups of having indeed found the one thing needful, I call this feeling, this consciousness of both the need for salvation and the

The Priesthood and Doctrine

reality of an answer to that need, as a living reality, a sense of soteriological urgency.

Soteriology has to do with the *soter*, the savior. In theology, soteriology is the doctrine of salvation. Any place where human beings ask life and death questions and where there is an urgent search for an answer to these questions, any place where an answer is made to such questions with the sense that upon one's choice, decision or action there hang the most weighty consequences, such a place, such a moment is marked by soteriological urgency. One can think of many places, and many ways, in which those questions are framed and answers are offered. This sense of the drama of salvation, of an answer to the problem of evil and suffering, can take many forms, personal, corporate, economic, social, political, and religious. One can see how it is impossible to find an answer to the cry of the human heart for an answer to these questions which concern us as matters of life and death that does not embrace in some ways all the dimensions of our existence. When the physician talks to the patient about the "options" for treatment, when someone gives a testimony about liberation from the disease of addiction thanks to the intervention of a "higher power," when young people fill the streets to protest policies they believe will lead to global ecological disaster, it is clear that we are in the presence of soteriological urgency, that an answer to the problem of salvation is being sought, and that a witness to the real possibility of salvation is being made with the utmost seriousness and with a demand for decision, commitment, and action as a matter of life or death.

Clearly the language of the Bible is a language of soteriological urgency. When Elijah defeats the prophets of Baal by calling down fire from heaven, the people are astounded and fall on their faces, and the words "choose this day whom ye shall serve, whether God or Baal" echo in their ears (1 Kings 18). The message of the prophets is that the one hope of Israel is that she should repent and return to the Lord. The Lord is her strength and her salvation; apart from God there is only ruin. "I had rather be a doorkeeper in the house of my God, than to dwell in the tents of wickedness" (Ps 84:10). Finally, the last of the prophets comes, and he says, "I indeed baptize you with water unto repentance: but he that cometh after me is mightier than I, whose shoes I am not worthy to bear: he shall baptize you with the Holy Ghost and with fire" (Matt 3:11). And that one when He comes speaks of selling everything for the pearl of great price, tells his disciples that they will only find their lives if they will lose them for His sake and for the Gospel. He bids them go now, this instant, for the harvest is heavy and the laborers are few. He warns them to keep watch for they do not know when the master of the house will return: "Watch, therefore, for ye know not what hour your Lord doth come" (Matt: 4:42).

The liturgies and formularies of the church, especially the Book of Common Prayer, because they are so replete with the language of scripture, are full of these words of Jesus that are urgent words, words of life and death, of that which may be found or lost, words of salvation and destruction. "You made us in your image but when we fell into evil and death you did not abandon us but sent your only and eternal Son. . . ." Christ has died, Christ is Risen, Christ will come again." "Do you renounce the evil powers which corrupt and destroy the creatures of God." "Will you turn to Jesus Christ and accept Him as your savior?" Will you follow and obey Him as your Lord?" "The blood of Christ which was shed for you preserve your body and soul unto everlasting life. . . ." "Ye that do truly and earnestly repent you of your sins and intend to lead the new life walking from hence forth in God's holy ways, draw near with faith and make your humble confession to almighty God devoutly kneeling."

All this: it leaps off every page of the Bible; it is the urgent voice of Jesus himself speaking to us out of every liturgy. Yet somehow, in much of our church life, much of the time, though the urgent words, words of life and death, of sin and salvation, are there, the tune is not. A true feeling for the words, a true consciousness of soteriological urgency, a recognition of the eschatological crisis which the presence of the Lord must create, this feeling, this consciousness, this music of both desperation and joy is absent.

How is it that the church has in so many instances lost this vital sense of the significance of its own life and teaching? Such a long story could be made of this, of telling how in the West the gift of God's reason has been turned into a weapon against the supernatural, of how the world has been split into a secular world of objective facts and a subjective world of beliefs, opinions and values, of how this subjective sphere of the sacred has become more and more private, more personal, more idiosyncratic, unreal and bizarre, how the churches have acquiesced in this tearing asunder of God's cosmos and have colluded in secularizing themselves and traded the mission of bringing to the world the objective saving presence of the living Lord for the mission of promoting "humane values" and being "centers of spirituality and inclusive community," of how the inhumanity, injustice, and immorality that are the natural consequence of the godforsaken world

The Priesthood and Doctrine

which secularism creates are used to further condemn and accuse the Christian message and God himself, of how, as C.S. Lewis says, God is now in the dock.

When it is said by confessing Christians, including the ordained servants of the church, that Jesus Christ is a way of salvation for me but not necessarily anyone else, it is a witness to the advance of a process by which the salvation of God as an objective fact that happened in Palestine, "under Pontius Pilate," and upon which the whole history of the human race hinges, has been turned into a private opinion and the inspiration for a merely personal spiritual journey. When such things are said by the ordained and consecrated teachers of the church, it is a witness that there is a deep crisis of confidence in the church about the truth of its teaching, about its doctrine as a saving doctrine.

At this point more is offered and with greater conviction in the basement of the church during the week than is offered in the sanctuary on Sunday morning. In such a case the words of salvation will continue to be used but they will indeed become a ritual in the worse sense of the word, a nostalgic reminder of what people used to believe and of a hope that once answered questions no longer being asked. Lassitude and ennui become the constant facts of life in such a church. To fill this emptiness, which comes from a lack of faith in our own teaching, our own doctrine, our own proclamation, the church will flee to other rhetoric about salvation and will constantly try to fan up a sense of urgency about the things of this world, as though they were the one thing needful and the salvation of humankind, and the life of the world to come. It is very tempting in such circumstances to resort to psychological tricks and emotional manipulation to keep at a fever pitch an artificially manufactured sense of religion.

There is a great need for a renewal of the role of doctrine within the life of the church. There is a need to reclaim the doctrine, the teaching of the church as a matter of life and death, as the means of making plain the urgent Word of salvation, the urgent reality of salvation that is in Jesus Christ, that meets the urgent search of the human heart for "a power greater than ourselves," that can save us from sure and certain destruction by a dark, canny, and destructive evil. There is a great need for the Christian priest whether bishop or presbyter, whether charged with the responsibility of teaching in a diocese or a parish, to regain a sense of the priesthood as an instrument of salvation and of the role of teaching sound doctrine as a role that has to do with matters of life and death, of salvation and destruction in this life and in the life of the world to come.

To Persevere in Love

The heart of the Christian faith is not teaching, not theology, but the crucified and risen Lord and the new life with the Father and with each other, this life that is a foretaste of the life of the world to come. But that presence, this opportunity to turn away from this world, which is passing away, and from the rulers of this world and toward the life of the world to come as that life comes to meet us in the Risen Lord, all this is brought to light, illuminated, made accessible, made into an understandable and necessary word of salvation, brought to light as a reality to which we would gladly surrender, brought to light as the living Word of life and light to those of us who are dying, by sound doctrine and by consecrated teaching.

A lot is made today of the fact that Anglicanism in general and the Episcopal Church in particular is not a "confessional" church, that doctrine is not what holds us together. All of this comes at the end of a long period during which there has been a tendency in the seminaries, entranced by secularism, materialism, and the historical-critical method to treat the doctrinal inheritance of the church as a collection of cultural artifacts and curiosities, as the telling title of one of the sections of the 1979 American Book of Common Prayer puts it, "historical documents." We are held together, it is said, by our worship and common prayer. It is said with some pride that unity of belief is not required of us. We find our unity in worship and "deeds, not creeds." Almost immediately this is said, monumental and revolutionary changes are proposed in liturgy, worship, and sacraments, changes that challenge the most fundamental historical consensus about basic Christian doctrines.

It is quite true that the English Reformers did not set up a confessional church in the same way that the Lutherans and the Calvinists did. It is also true that both the majority of the clergy and laity of the Church of England came to be revolted by the violent and uncharitable controversy leading up to the Elizabethan settlement and gladly accepted the Book of Common Prayer and the modest, by Reformation standards, explication of the Thirty-Nine Articles as sufficient formularies of unity. It is true that because of this history there developed an ethos of granting the greatest possible latitude to conscience (assuming of course, that the conscience in question was formed and informed by the Scriptures, the liturgies, and the great teaching tradition of the Church), and of accepting actions, a willingness to sign the articles, a willingness to use and pray the offices of the Prayer Book as sufficient, and purposively allow for some finessing of definition in order to comprehend the greatest unity possible. It may be that of all

The Priesthood and Doctrine

Christian churches, Anglicans have practiced the art of a diplomatic language of theology. At times this has made possible a respect for conscience and a maintenance of community other churches have missed. At times it makes us liable to cynical obfuscation.

It is not right to say that we are not a doctrinal church. I doubt there can really be such a thing. There is no way of salvation of which I am aware that does not have a teaching, a doctrine. In our church basements, week in and week out a saving doctrine is proclaimed with great confidence and conviction as a sure guide to a 'spiritual experience" which can save one from destruction by the disease of addiction. Many of the paths of salvation that are offered today are notorious for the complexity and tediousness of their doctrine. So the comedian can make a good living telling jokes about what it means to be politically correct. There is no salvation without doctrine. Indeed some paths of salvation appear to consist only of doctrine and teaching. There is no authentic form of Christianity that is without doctrine, though the purpose of the doctrine is to point away from itself and toward Christ.

It is just plain false and dishonest to say that we are not a doctrinal church. All versions of the Christian faith are doctrinal. They have doctrine, authoritative teaching of the Lord, of Christ Himself, and they have doctrine, authoritative teaching about Christ and about the salvation which He brings. All the extant Books of Common Prayer ring with such doctrine on every page, the teaching of the Bible itself, in its own words, the teachings of the Lord Himself in His own words, "Come unto me all ye that travail and are heavy laden and I will give you rest" (Matt 11:28), and very explicit, straightforward teachings about Him and the meaning of the salvation to be found in Him: " We believe in one God and in His only begotten Son," "Very God from very God, begotten not made, of one being with the Father," "who for us and for our salvation was crucified under Pontius Pilate." "We believe in the resurrection of the dead, the forgiveness of sins and the life of the world to come."

Baptism, Eucharist, Ordination, Prayers for the Sick, Holy Matrimony, Burial, all these contain a great deal of explicit doctrinal teaching of the most traditional sort, often self-consciously reaching back and bringing forward the insights of the Patristic period. There is even more doctrine that is implicit, as in the place given to the Eucharist in the American prayer book of 1979. Anglicanism (and the Episcopal Church is no exception) in its prayer books and formularies is highly doctrinal. To say that it is not is to turn a blind eye and a deaf ear to the words that echo in our common prayer and to deny their plain meaning and the documented intention of those who were authorized to craft them on our behalf.

It is a very dishonest thing to claim that we are not a doctrinal church. Those who make this claim do so not because they want to propose a doctrineless Christianity; such a thing is not possible, but because they wish to be released from some of the particular doctrines of the church, so that they may embrace some other doctrines, often doctrines that are alien and hostile to the teaching of the Apostles, for instance that there is no resurrection of the body, or that Christ is a way rather than the way, the truth, and the life. To profess the traditional doctrine is not to trade a "worship centered" Christianity for a doctrine centered or confessional church life. To cease to profess the doctrinal tradition is simply to trade a church life loyal to the teaching of the Apostles for a church life based on some other teaching which must necessarily be the doctrine of a salvation other than the salvation found in Jesus Christ.

Jesus Christ is the Apostle and the high priest of God. He brings the living reality of salvation. He is completely consecrated to true teaching about the identity of God, "Truly, Truly, I say to you. . . ." He teaches us about the goodness of God, about God's care for each person, explicitly: "Not a sparrow falls but your Father knows it, are you not worth more than these?" (Matt 10:29,31). He teaches the same doctrine in parable, such as the parable about the man who had one hundred sheep and left the ninety-nine to go in search of the one (Luke 15:4). And He teaches a doctrine about God by His actions, and especially by His treatment of sinners and His fellowship with them. He has a terrible and awesome doctrine about the seriousness of sin, about the lost vocation of the people of Israel, about how sin is to be forgiven and Israel renewed and restored to her place in God's plan of salvation as "the light of the nations." The Messiah must suffer and die, that is the Lord's teaching and doctrine, and the Apostles reject it. When Peter tempts the Lord to abandon His doctrine, the saving truth that He has come not only to teach but to be and to accomplish, Jesus calls him Satan. On His way to the cross, the Lord has harsh words of condemnation for the false and distorted teaching of the Pharisees and religious leaders who by false and insincere teaching lead the people astray. After His resurrection, on the road to Emmaus, He walks with two disciples, teaching them, opening to them the scriptures, helping them to see the meaning of the salvation wrought in His death and resurrection. He promises the Holy

The Priesthood and Doctrine

Spirit who shall lead them into all truth. He commissions them to go into all the world to make disciples, in other words to teach a doctrine, and what they are to teach is not their own but their witness to His teaching, which He gave them by word and by His death and rising again. The priesthood of Jesus Christ includes an absolute consecration to a saving doctrine about who God is, who God's Messiah is, and what God is doing in Him for the sake of a lost world. This consecration is in the blood of the cross.

When the Risen Lord breathes upon His disciples after the resurrection, He gives them His Apostolate: "As the Father sends me, even so I send you" (John 20:21). They are witnesses to the living and risen Lord, to who He is and what God has done in and through Him for the salvation of the world. Their consecration to Him as Apostles and priests includes a consecration to be stewards of a definitive teaching, a definitive doctrine about God, about Jesus, about the need of humanity for costly salvation that is to be had by an encounter with the Risen Lord as He makes Himself known in the Life of His body, the church. Thus the Apostle Paul warns in Galatians 1:8, "But though we, or an angel from heaven, preach any other gospel unto you than that which we have preached," do not believe it. In the Bible, in the life, death, and resurrection of Jesus, in the ministry of the Apostles, the matter of true doctrine is a matter of life and death, of salvation. To be in the Apostolic succession, to be a priest, is to be a person of doctrine, a person who can give a confident teaching that clearly points the way to a real and effective salvation, a person not who teaches with detachment and irony about historical curiosities, but one who answers the urgent questions of the human heart with an equally urgent, true, and trustworthy word, with trustworthy words about the Lord and trustworthy words of the Lord.

The Reformation was a moment when the seriousness of true doctrine was rediscovered, when the power of false doctrine and false teaching to lead people astray and to hide and obscure the salvation of Christ, rather than to bring it to light, was disclosed. The Reformers perceived that the odious doctrine of indulgences and sinecures obscured the goodness of God and the grace of salvation and caused people to fall either into a false complacency and impious reliance on works, or to fall into despair because they knew they could not atone for their own sins nor ever balance the books of their lives no matter how many good deeds they did or indulgences they bought.

The ordinal of the 1979 Book of Common Prayer is a beautiful and profound rite, and is an example of the positive impact of the liturgical movement in the life of the church. It represents a repristination of the liturgy, reaching back to liturgical forms that come from the witness of the Patristic Age. The ordination rite in the 1979 Book brings out very strongly the reality of the Body of Christ and the interdependence and mutual relationships in the one Body between the different orders of ministry. The actual formula for ordination was rightly recognized to be a prayer together with the laying on of hands. For the formula "take thou authority" the prayer for ordination was substituted, for the long exhortation on the ordained ministry was substituted a succinct teaching on the Apostolic succession, the Body of Christ, the three orders of ordained ministers, and the role of the ordained in service to the church. Anything that could possibly lead to an inappropriate clericalism was edited out. There has been great gain in all of this, but in the process the note of seriousness and weightiness of preaching and teaching Apostolic doctrine, which is a very distinctive element of all the Books of Common Prayer from 1549 through the American book of 1928, has become muted. Let us recall some of these words from the old book which remain little changed from Cranmer's original. In my view, we are more threatened by a forgetfulness of the office of the sound teaching of Apostolic doctrine than we are by an exaggerated clericalism.

You cannot read the service in the 1662 book without being struck by the way in which it drives home the significance of the work of the ordained ministry in the salvation of souls and the significance of teaching and preaching in that work. Over and over the ordinand is urged to look to his (sic) doctrine. The opening collect prays that God who by the Holy Spirit has appointed "divers orders of ministers" would replenish the ordinands with "the truth of Thy doctrine" and with "innocency of life." But perhaps the most remarkable part of the 1662 service is the exhortation which preceeds the examination. It persisted in the American church with little change through the 1928 book. In the exhortation there is a sense of the solemnity of the office being conferred, a very intense sense of soteriological urgency, "Now again we exhort, in the Name of Our Lord Jesus Christ, that ye have in remembrance, into how high an dignity, and to how weighty an office and charge ye are called: that is to say, to be messengers, watchmen and stewards of the Lord; to teach and to premonish, to feed and provide for the Lord's family; to seek for Christ's sheep that are dispersed abroad, and for his children who are in the midst of this naughty world, that they may be saved by Christ forever. Have always therefore printed in your remembrance, how great a treasure is committed to your charge. For

The Priesthood and Doctrine

they are the sheep of Christ, which He bought with His death and for which He shed His Blood. . . ." And so it goes in the most solemn way beseeching earnest labor, warning of the horrible punishment that will ensue from any negligence of office and urging that the priest persevere in bringing all the people of the parish, "unto that agreement in the faith and knowledge of God, and to that ripeness and perfectness of age in Christ, that there be no place left among you, either for error in religion or for viciousness of life." Here there is a vision for a personal, pastoral, sacrificial parish priesthood which has a care and concern for the teaching of sound doctrine and the religious understanding of the people at the very heart of it. The connection between "error in religion" and "viciousness of life" is taken for granted. It is assumed that good and sound teaching helps people to grow into the full stature of Christ, and that erroneous conceptions of God, of the savior, of the path of salvation cannot help but result in personal immorality and parish discord.

The exhortation goes on to make the obvious point that such a ministry is impossible without the grace of God and bids the ordinand pray for the Holy Spirit, "and seeing that ye cannot by any other means compass the doing of so weighty a work, pertaining to the salvation of man, but with doctrine and exhortation taken out of the Holy Scriptures, and with a life agreeable to the same, consider how studious ye ought to be in reading and learning the scriptures and in framing the manners both of yourselves, and them that specially pertain unto you, according to the rule of the same scriptures; and for this self-same cause, how ye ought to forsake and set aside, as much as ye may, all worldly cares and studies." The exhortation continues with a call that "as much as lieth in you, ye will apply yourselves wholly to this one thing, and draw all your cares and studies this way;" And further, "that by daily reading and weighing of the scriptures, ye may wax riper and stronger in your ministry."

Teaching, scripture, doctrine, a personal and pastoral interest in the people with a view to their eternal souls, a life-long commitment to develop and grow in understanding and as a teacher of truth, and by God's grace to lead the people into maturity of faith and out of any "error in religion or viciousness of life;" these are the components of the vision of the priesthood the old ordinal gives. The priest who is a pastor with a real care of souls must be a profound student of the scriptures and a teacher of sound doctrine.

To Persevere in Love

Then comes the examination in which the significance of teaching out of scripture is reiterated. Promises are exacted to minister the "doctrine and sacraments and discipline that you may teach the people committed to your charge with all diligence to keep and observe the same."

Then this, "Will you be ready, with all faithful diligence to banish and drive away from the church all erroneous and strange doctrines contrary to God's Word; and to use both public and private monitions and exhortation, as well to the sick as to the whole, within your Cures, as need shall require, and occasion be given?" The commentaries on the Book of Common Prayer note that the inclusion of this promise in the form for ordination to the priesthood adds to that order a responsibility that was found in the medieval ordinals only in the service for the consecration of bishops. Evidently the framers of the Prayer Book wanted to magnify both the authority and the responsibility of the parish priest for the stewardship of Apostolic doctrine and for the unity of the people in faith.

This is our heritage, and the historical and theological roots of the Prayer Book vision of Holy Orders. Each age emphasizes themes that seem particularly needful in the life of the church at that time. The 1979 Book emphasizes in a very beautiful way the themes of the Body of Christ and the role of the ordained ministry within the interdependent life of the one Body. This is in the foreground, along with the significance of the pastoral and liturgical function, but the note of sound teaching is still there. When in the 1979 Book the bishop gives the ordinand the Bible as a sign of authority to preach the Word of God and to administer His Holy Sacraments and says, "Do not forget the trust committed to you as a priest of the Church of God," we are well-advised to hear those words of Cranmer from the 1662 exhortation laying out for us the weighty and solemn nature of that trust, and our need to be teachers of sound, wholesome and Biblical doctrine.

But what is this doctrine? Where is it to be found? If you say the Bible, how can you get around the wide variety of legitimate interpretation and settle on any kind of authoritative teaching? We have no confession, no magisterium, so how can a vision of sound teaching of authoritative doctrine be made plausible?

Yet, the ordinals of all the Books of Common Prayer, including those presently in use, exact a promise from the ordinand that implies that there is such a thing as sound teaching and saving doctrine, and that to be a teacher, professor, and defender of that doctrine is at the heart of the office to which we are ordained. The ordinals do not belabor the content of

The Priesthood and Doctrine

the doctrine but take it for granted that it is discernible to a person who has met the canonical requirements, and that in the time leading up to ordination, the bishop who is the premier steward of doctrine will have been satisfied with the ordinand's capacity to teach the orthodox faith. That commissions on ministry are often more interested in more topical issues does not change the weight and responsibility that is upon us to set forth the doctrine of salvation.

At the very least we are committed to teach and explicate the doctrine that is explicitly and implicitly taught in the liturgies of Baptism and Holy Eucharist, as for example, in the recitation of the Nicene Creed in the Eucharist or the Apostles' Creed in Baptism, as well as what is implied and what is enacted in the liturgical performance of these two fundamental sacraments.

Especially in the Holy Eucharist, the sacrament toward which, as St. Thomas says, the priesthood is ordered, there is in all of the Eucharistic prayers a recitation of the mighty deeds of God culminating in the sending of the eternal Son to be our salvation. There is, without doubt, take any view of Eucharistic sacrifice that you please, a presentation of His death on Calvary as an atoning, sacrificial death. There is an explicit proclamation of His resurrection and a prayer for the gift of His Spirit, "that we might receive all the benefits of His passion. . . .That He might dwell in us and we in Him." There is even a specific and explicit liturgical reference to the Apocalypse and the expectation that the Lord will come at the end of time to bring in the Kingdom in power and glory.

Implicitly, explicitly, and in the enacted presentation of the liturgical action, there is summarized and represented the whole doctrine, the whole Apostolic teaching about God, humanity, about creation, the fall and sin, about the providence of God in choosing Israel, about the revelation of the Word of God in the law and the prophets, about in the fullness of time the Incarnation of the Son of God from the flesh of the Virgin Mary by the power of the Holy Spirit, of the teaching and healing of Jesus, of His atoning and saving death, of His Resurrection, Ascension, gift of the Spirit, and His coming in glory, of the judgment of the quick and the dead, of the resurrection of the body and the life of the world to come. It cannot be that we are commissioned to say these great words which ring with the preaching of the Apostles and echoing voices of the whole history of Christian thought and feeling at the altar without also being obligated to a deep contemplation of this doctrine, and being obligated to teach this doctrine in and to the church.

There is a moment in the traditional Anglo-Catholic ceremonial of the Eucharist taken over from the Latin rite, when after the offertory and before proceeding to the canon of the mass, the priest washes his hands. A so-called "secret prayer" is said that is a quote from Psalm 26: "I wash my hands in the water of innocence that I may go about the altar of my God reciting His mighty deeds of salvation." The recitation, the representation of the whole doctrine of salvation from creation to the parousia is at the heart of the priestly life.

This means that just as the liturgy does not leave out any of the well-known chapters of the story of the creation, the fall, and redemption, neither may we. A priest may not present the goodness of creation in such a way as to leave out the teaching of the reality of the evil one, the fall, and the struggle with sin. The Word of love made known to us in the Incarnation may not be presented without the cross, the cross may not be presented without the resurrection, nor the resurrection without the ascension and the gift of the Spirit. The mystery of Christ may not be presented apart from the mystery of the church, the meaning of the holy order of the church and the sacraments. The call to mission and ministry in this life may not be presented apart from the judgment upon this world that is passing away and the hope of the world to come. We are consecrated to bring forth the whole story of the mighty deeds of God from Genesis to Revelation, and the whole meaning of this story by setting forth the doctrines of creation, fall, redemption, and what has been called the last things, when God shall bring to completion His work of love and glory. This lays upon the priest the greatest obligation to comprehend the wholeness of the story and the meaning of the story explicated in the great doctrines of the church, to see the interrelatedness of the story and the interdependence of the chapters, to perceive the distortion that creeps into the life of a church, whether a local parish or one of the historic denominations when some part of the story is emphasized at the expense of some other part. The priest is also obligated to perceive the distortion that creeps into the life of the priest and of individual parishioners when a vision of the wholeness of the faith or the catholicity of doctrine is lost.

In each particular context, in each locality, in each age, there are elements of the story, there are particular doctrinal themes that resonate with the people. There are particular elements of the story and particular doctrinal themes that resonate in the heart of the individual priest. Often a priest has a particular gift for bringing out some feature of the great story, some aspect of its doctrinal significance, especially well and with great power. This is to be celebrated but it also points the priest to a challenge to find the depth of the priestly office in the struggle to bring forward the wholeness of the trustworthy Words of God, and the wholeness of the trustworthy words about God in the great tradition of the church, and so to light the path to a more complete and profound experience of the saving grace of God.

In the great Christological debates that led up to the creeds of Nicaea and Chalcedon, there were moments when the divinity of Christ was stressed to such a degree that His humanity began to disappear, and so also began to disappear His sympathy with the human race and His capacity to save what He had assumed. At other times the humanity was stressed to such a degree that Jesus was in danger of becoming a purely this-worldly figure, another wise man and teacher who gives yet one more impossible standard to follow, and the mighty act of God in the incarnation and atonement, that new life with its power and virtue, begins to be lost. There are times when the reality of the fall and sin and the Holy God's judgment upon sin are stressed to such a degree that the vision of the goodness of the creation and the mercy of God are brought into question. In our own day we suffer from an attempt to bypass the fall, the reality of sin, and the need for redemption. The inherent goodness of the creation and human nature is stressed to such a degree that it sometimes appears that the church exists to proclaim to humanity that men and women are already blessed and redeemed and need only to have it pointed out to them. On account of this, a new, stern, and unmerciful works righteousness is being introduced. People are once again told that they need only try harder to do better in their struggle with evil, which is conceived of as mistaken ideas. How much more realistic, even biblical, the language about "our lives have become unmanageable," and the necessity to "believe in a higher power who can restore us to sanity."

If the priests of the church do not teach the whole and wholesome doctrine of Christ and truly open the way, illuminate the path, to a saving encounter with Christ, people will go in search of a doctrine that recognizes the urgency of the human situation and which speaks an urgent word of life and death in reply.

To Persevere in Love

So He asks them, "Will you now also turn away and leave me?" And the answer comes, "Lord, to whom shall we go? For you have the words of eternal life" (John 6:67,68). He has given us these words so that we might give them to others that they and we should have life in His name. At the heart of the priestly vocation is the mission to hand on faithfully and loyally the doctrine of Christ and His Apostles, those trustworthy words of the Savior and those trustworthy words about Him.

6

The Priesthood and Sacrifice [1]

THERE HAS BEEN A tremendous ambivalence about the priesthood the whole time that I've been ordained. It's understandable that there should be some ambivalence and hostility towards the priesthood outside of the church, but there has been a crisis of identity about the priesthood within the church. Sometimes that masquerades as a concern for Reformation theology. There is a legitimate concern that we should not have an understanding of the ordained function in the church that somehow obscures the once and for all sacrifice of Christ and His office as the one and only priest and mediator between God and the human race. Sometimes it masquerades as a concern for egalitarianism. We have anxiety about not being democratic enough. While both of these are appropriate concerns, they can at times be camouflage for a simple allergy to anything that witnesses to the reality of the supernatural.

I want to make a case for the centrality of the category of sacrifice to understanding the ordained ministerial priesthood in the church of God. I believe attending to the properly sacrificial nature of the ministerial priesthood does not obscure the one sufficient sacrifice of Christ and His office as the one priest and mediator between God and humanity but rather is the God-ordained means for keeping the church dependent on that one sacrifice and on her great high priest.

Now, first of all, what is a sacrifice? What was it that those Old Testament priests did, those levitical priests, when they went into the temple?

---

1. These thoughts first took shape in the ordination sermon for the priesting of the Rev. John Mason Lock, May 9, 2009, All Souls Church, Oklahoma City, Oklahoma.

The levitical priests took the blood of an animal, and they poured the blood out upon the altar. So, a sacrifice is a pouring out, and it's a pouring out of life. In the Old Testament, people understood that the life of the animal, the life of the person, resided in the blood. What the priest did was to pour out this life, and it was felt that this pouring out of this life made an atonement, that it made amends for man's offense to God and that in some way, in some mysterious way, it cleansed or purified. In the Old Testament, blood is a very interesting thing: on the one hand, it makes people dirty; on the other hand, it makes them clean. And what was the purpose of all that? The purpose of all that was the re-consecrating of the people.

God had a plan to bring his wayward children home, and his plan was to have a people that would live towards him in such a way and live towards each other in such a way that all the other peoples of the earth would look to that people, his people, and say, "surely your God is the true God; tell us about him that we might also know him and love him and serve him." When they wandered away from the way of life that they were given, God gave them a system, this sacrificial system, the tabernacle and then the temple in Jerusalem, which involved blood sacrifice. And the purpose of the blood sacrifice, the purpose of pouring out the lives of these animals on the altar, was that the people should be cleansed and re-consecrated, made new, made again into God's holy and righteous people. They were called to be that; they had wandered away from that; they needed to be gathered into that; they needed to be re-consecrated, set apart again, and they needed to be made clean. That was the liturgy of the priests of the Old Testament. The writer to the Hebrews tells us that the blood of the goats and the bulls availeth nothing. It was all a kind of education, it was all a kind of pointing forward to the priest who is to come. Jesus Christ is that priest, the one who is able to do what the priests of the Old Testament were charged to do and yet could not do, and that is to really and truly cleanse the people, redeem and renew them, re-consecrate them as a holy nation and a kingdom of priests. What was not possible to accomplish by pouring out the lives of innumerable animals, Jesus Christ has actually accomplished by pouring his life out to His Father for our sake and pouring His life out to us for His Father's sake.

When it is said that the ordained priest in the church is indeed a priest who offers sacrifice, it is not being said that the priest does something above, beyond, apart from the one sacrifice of Jesus Christ. In the Christian church, anything that is done is done by Jesus Christ. If there is teaching,

The Priesthood and Sacrifice

He is the one who teaches. If there is forgiveness which is on offer, He is the one who is offering the forgiveness. If there is healing, it is His touch that is the healing touch. If enemies are reconciled, He is the one who reconciles. If peace is given, it is His peace. So, whether it is lay ministry or ordained ministry or any other kind of ministry, there is nothing that is done in the church that Jesus doesn't do; by the power of the Spirit in His body the church, He does those things. He continues to do those things which He did when He walked among us. So, there is no question of the ordained Christian priest adding in any way to the one perfect and sufficient sacrifice of the Savior, that the Savior offers. That's not what is happening when the ordained priest offers the sacrifice of praise and thanksgiving in the Eucharist.

We have been waiting; the people of God have been waiting for *the* priest to come who can really reconcile us to the Father, who can really make us clean. There is an old Gospel song, "Nothing but the blood of Jesus." What is this? It's this life of His that is poured out in praise and adoration towards the Father, and towards us in love and service. This pouring out of His life, it is this sacrifice that renews us and consecrates us and makes us clean. Titus says it this way (we hear this in the appointed epistle for the first Eucharist of Christmas) "to make for himself, to consecrate for himself a holy people zealous of good works" (2:14). The purpose of *the* priest is to do that work, it is to reconcile and return God's lost children to the Father and to consecrate them as a holy people zealous for good works. The whole Old Testament system was pointing towards this until He who is *the* priest, really the one and only priest, until He should come. He is the Light of the world. He is the bread of life. He is living water. He is the Good Shepherd. He is the priest. He is also that Lamb of God that was slain, as Charles Wesley's hymn says, "priest and victim in the Eucharistic feast." So, when we are saying that the ordained priest offers sacrifice, we're not saying that something is being offered in addition to the sacrifice of Christ, and we're not saying that something is being offered other than what Jesus accomplished on Calvary or continues to plead before the Father in the heavenly session. We are saying that the ministerial priesthood is completely identified with and makes visible in the midst of the Church the one complete sacrifice and the eternal priesthood of her Savior.

The personal God is not content that the sacrifice of His Son, that what Jesus Christ has done, by the pouring out of His life to bring men and women back to their Father, to make them again clean and holy, and to give them a witness in the world which shall cause the rest of God's alienated children to come home, should be a story in a book somewhere. The personal God wants that sacrifice to become as tangible in our time as it was on Calvary; he wants it to become contemporary and personal; he wants it to become something that people can see and touch, that is put in front of people in such a way that they can respond to it, that their hearts can be broken and made warm so that they can be reconciled to their Father and give their lives anew to God in Christ, and receive the power of the Holy Spirit, and be witnesses in His Name to the ends of the earth. And so, God calls individuals to the ordained priesthood. The Lord calls in His Church and through His Church. He comes to His Church with the marks of the crucifixion upon Him, this crucified and risen one, and He breathes into His Church. He puts His Spirit in us. He says, "My peace I give you; as the Father sent me, so I send you" (John 20:21). The twelve are called to continue the ministry of their master. And so it is the will of the Lord that in this time and in this place, this particular person whom He calls should come and give over their life to a particular form of service, to a particular form of identification with the Savior for the sake of the people in order that the sacrifice of Christ might be re-presented in front of His people in such a way that it is contemporary, personal, and real for them and provokes their response. The response as a holy people, as a kingdom of priests, is the light to the nations that is meant to guide all the Father's wayward children home. Representing the one priest to the priestly people so that they may be renewed in their vocation and mission is the essence of the ordained priesthood.

This is the way of the Bible: God always calls the many through the one. We should be very surprised if all of a sudden the system were changed in the New Testament. People not only need to hear about what God has done, but they need to have someone take them by the hand and put their hand in the hand of the Master. That is what the ordained priesthood is all about. And so, in certain times, in certain places, amongst a certain set of God's people, God calls this person and that person. This is the meaning of that old word, the parson-- it just means the person. This is the person that God has called that He might call many through this one. This is His plan, that the sacrifice of His Son might be re-presented.

It is entirely accurate to say that the ordained priesthood is a priesthood that offers sacrifice, but when we say that, evangelicals should not take offense. We're saying that Jesus Christ is the only priest. He is the one

The Priesthood and Sacrifice

who does everything that is to be done, and those called to ordained ministerial priesthood are but instruments in His hands.

Now when the sacrifice of Jesus Christ is re-presented, whether in the prayer of consecration at the Eucharist or in the preaching of the Gospel (they are equally priestly acts), it evokes the challenge of response for us: we have to respond. And this is another strange thing. We can't do anything of our own, we can't do anything for our own salvation, but whatever we do, the faith we have, the good works that we do, all of our response to God is not us but Christ who worketh in us; it is the gift of the Holy Spirit. And yet, we have to give ourselves to this. We give ourselves to the sacrifice of Christ in the church in ways that are appropriate to our order. I see three elements to that response that are particularly appropriate and mark the life of the ordained priest.

Austin Farrer, the great Anglican theologian, says that the clergy are "walking sacraments."[2] So, first of all, the ordained priest re-presents, as a walking sacrament, the one perfect and sufficient sacrifice of the Lord. And then, he responds with his own sacrifice, and it has a shape. And the first element of the shape of that sacrifice is that it is a sacrifice of poverty of spirit. All Christians are called to this, but the ordained have it in a particularly intense way. They cannot get away from it; they are tied to it. This is what happens in the rite of ordination. A person is being bound by irrevocable promises to the ministerial priesthood; one can never get away from it after this. One can be a good priest, one can be a bad priest, one can be a failed priest, but one can never get away from it. It's an awesome thing. And poverty of spirit is a sacrifice that is demanded of the priest. When you enter into the ordained ministry, you become very, very aware, as St. Paul says, that we have this treasure in earthen vessels (2 Cor 4:7), and that nothing that you are and that nothing you can do amounts to anything. And that the call is to be nobody and nothing and to come and die.

We had a rather wealthy man who came to the seminary where I teach. We were really hoping that he might help us with our work. He said to me, "Do the brightest and the best and the most accomplished come to your school?" And I didn't know how to answer; I really didn't know how to answer. We get incredible people at the school. I've had a retired state department official; I've had a professor of finance; I've had people that could do anything in any graduate school in the country. And I've had people who have found school very, very difficult. And they were all called

2. Farrer, *Austin Farrer: The Essential Sermons*, 101.

by God. And they all were giving themselves away to Jesus Christ. I didn't know how to explain to this man that this ministry is really not about accomplishment. If you do anything, it is not you who do it. And the most essential part of what you are called to do is nothing that is possible in the flesh; it's not humanly possible.

This is a call to be a failure; this is a call to know your own unworthiness, to plumb the depths of it. This is a call to plumb the depths of your own inadequacy. This is a call to be nobody and nothing. And the flesh chafes against this. The flesh in the Bible means humanly. In our frail humanity we want to be somebody and something. Being human, every once in a while, a priest will wake up and say, "Today, I am going to be somebody and something." And, of course, everybody sees that the priest in question is a complete and utter contradiction because Jesus Christ did not grasp equality with God but humbled himself, and Christ is glorified, even by contradiction. As a priest of the church you are his witness, and you re-present his sacrifice; willingly or unwillingly, you cannot get away from it. So this is one aspect of sacrifice, poverty of spirit.

Another aspect of the sacrifice is a sacrifice of intercession. Jesus Christ was an interceder; he intercedes for us yet. Because we don't celebrate the feast of the Ascension well enough in the church, we may lose track of the heavenly session where he yet intercedes for us. One thing that happens to ordained priests, especially in pastoral ministry, is that they see more than they can ever possibly do anything about. Now at the seminary we try to teach people to be good counselors; we try to teach them about how grief works, and to be a good companion to people as they are going through grief. We try to teach them how to be crisis counselors and to have a kind of minimum competency. But it will never be enough. It's not possible that it will ever be enough. A priest will see every day, day in and day out, so many things that the priest can do nothing about other than to hold up Christ and to pray and to intercede. And after you've been doing it for a while, you see the train wreck coming. You see what's going on in this family now, and you know what's going to happen with the teenagers down the road. You see what's going on with this couple now, and you know what's going to happen in five or six years. You see how the parents are treating their children, and you know they are going to die alone and unhappy. So many things you see, you can't do a thing about. But, what is the priest in the Old Testament? He stands before the people with God on his heart, and he stands before God with the people on his heart (Exod 39:14). To be ordained is to be tied to

The Priesthood and Sacrifice

intercession in a way that is irrevocable and unavoidable, and to see things over and over again, day in and day out about which one can do nothing but pray. It is a persistent formation that brings you again and again to the place of intercession. This powerlessness and grief is a sacrifice, a sacrifice of intercession.

And finally, there is a dimension to the ordained priesthood that can be called a sacrifice of surrender. There was a particular form of the sacrifice of Jesus Christ: He put Himself completely and totally in His Father's hands on that night in the garden of Gethsemane. He put himself completely and totally in His Father's hands, and the way that he did that was to put himself completely and totally in the hands of His people. What is the passion of Jesus Christ? The passion of Jesus Christ is that He came to His own and His own knew Him not; He was despised and rejected. There is a vulnerability of the priest to the people that is irrevocable, and that is very awesome, and very frightening. The priest is at the mercy of the people. You will be loved. There will be people who love you. But the newly ordained priest is not going to exercise ministry for even an hour before there will be somebody who will be unhappy, before there will be somebody who will be angry. The psychologist says we shouldn't pay too much attention to that; we should pay attention to the positive, take in more of the positive. Well yes, there could be a psychological defect in dwelling on the negative, but should the ordained priest try to avoid the passion of the Good Shepherd who came to His own and His own knew Him not? He persevered toward us with love, though we despised and rejected Him and drove Him out of our lives and onto the cross. So must the ordained priest persevere in love.

The priesthood demands a kind of complete surrender of our lives into the hands of the people we serve. We are at their mercy, as the Lord put Himself at our mercy. Now, one thing that happens at the seminary about January of the last year of seminary, students begin to intuit the terrible vulnerability that comes with ordination, and it's the cause of a lot of cold feet. A lot of students start thinking that, "gee, a couple more years of graduate education appears very attractive at this point" or "maybe I could go into chaplaincy work" or "maybe I could work in the world and work in the church part-time." Is there just something that I can do to make ordination something that the human heart can bear? And the answer is no. The answer is no. There is no escape, once these promises have been made, once these prayers have been said, once the bishop lays on hands—there is no going back. So there is sacrifice required: a sacrifice of poverty of spirit; a sacrifice of intercession; a sacrifice of surrender.

To those of us who are ordained, I say it is indeed our ministry to offer sacrifice, to present before the people the one full, perfect, and sufficient sacrifice of the Master, and present it before them in such a way that it is real to them and that it breaks their hearts and makes them new. Let us give ourselves whole-heartedly to the sacrifices of poverty of spirit and of intercession and of surrender. Let us carry about in our bodies the marks of the suffering and death of Christ, that His risen life might also appear in us, and we may be His faithful witness until the day we die.

7

The Power and Dignity of the Priesthood[1]

MUCH HAS BEEN WRITTEN about the perception of a crisis in the priesthood. The Cornerstone Project was developed by the Episcopal Church Foundation in order to help strengthen ordained leadership at a time when clergy are reporting themselves to be discouraged, confused, and highly stressed. One of the most recent findings of the Cornerstone Project is that the parish priests in the project had difficulty articulating a theology of priesthood. The staff found that the priests in the project could discuss theological readings with competence but that when they spoke about their parish ministries they did not tend to speak in theological categories. I was one of a group of clergy, theologians, and Cornerstone staff who attended a conference at the College of Preachers in June of 1995 to attempt to understand the meaning of this finding and to suggest a course of action. The thoughts that I am going to share with you tonight represent my contribution to that discussion.

While there are many practical problems in the parish ministry which must be addressed, it is my conviction that the fundamental stress, the fundamental crisis is a crisis of meaning. There is a genuine confusion about the meaning of priesthood in the minds of the priests, bishops, deacons, and laity. What does it mean to be a priest? What is the work of a priest?

---

1. A talk given at the Annual Meeting of The Society for the Increase of the Ministry at Trinity College, Hartford, Connecticut, November 1, 1995. Subsequently published in *Sewanee Theological Review*, 43.2. Reprinted by permission of the author and the publisher.

67

This question dogs us to such a degree that the question, "Do we really need priests?" is a question seriously asked today. Perhaps you have heard of the cutting edge liturgical practice of celebrating the Eucharist by putting the elements in the midst of the assembly and reciting the prayer of consecration as a group as a way of witnessing to the priesthood of all believers. This kind of activity points toward a crisis in the understanding of the meaning of the priesthood, indeed in the meaning of the church itself.

I had a vivid experience of this crisis of meaning at a recent clergy gathering in my home diocese of Connecticut. At the first clergy conference we had with our newly elected diocesan bishop, there was a great discussion of the number of hours a priest should work per week. This discussion generated more heat than light. It was clear to me that the topic touched the parish clergy in a tender place and that none of the Bishop's kind and prudential advice about an appropriate work week seemed to console or satisfy. I realized that the question being answered, "How much should I work?" was not the question really being asked. That question was, "Does my work have meaning?" In a growing parish with good finances and improving membership the question of meaning seems to have an obvious answer. Many clergy serve in places where despite persistent and dedicated effort there is little observable result in terms of growing revenue and membership. What does it mean to pour out your life in such a ministry? Does it make a difference? If so, what is the difference that it makes?

Whence cometh this confusion? A number of factors converge. There has been a change in the society. There is the much discussed post-modern, post-Christian society in which the church as an institution has become increasingly marginalized. There is the generation shift, the change in values, the consumer mindset of the baby boomers whose loyalty must be constantly re-won. There is much good discussion of the exterior forces that converge to challenge our understanding of parish ministry and priesthood. These must be taken seriously and they require a response. But all these issues simply exacerbate the underlying confusion about the theological meaning of priesthood. One of the reasons the church and its ordained ministry are having trouble responding effectively to the change in social context is a lack of conviction about what is essential about holy orders and the life of the church. I want to limit my remarks to the theological sources of the confusion. We have no hope of responding effectively to the sea change in the context of the church without an inner clarity about the nature and meaning of holy orders and the church.

The Power and Dignity of the Priesthood

But what is it that keeps us from being clear? What confuses us? We are confused about soteriology, the doctrine of salvation. There is no soteriological consensus in the church today. For some, salvation is rescue from divine retribution by confessing dependence on the blood sacrifice of Jesus on the cross. For some, salvation is the pursuit of a spiritual journey. For some, salvation is a metaphor for social justice or psychological wholeness. Most of the popular images of salvation treat the church and its ministry as accessories before or after the fact of salvation. The locus of salvation is elsewhere; at the revival or the charismatic conference, at the meeting of the women's caucus, at the retreat, or the conference on spirituality. We don't know what salvation is, and we are looking for it almost anywhere but in the parish church, and we expect almost anyone to be its minister save the parish priest. The result is that we inhabit the forms of the church without understanding their meaning. The church becomes increasingly merely a secular organization. It ceases to be holy, sacred, the sacrament of the new life in Jesus Christ, what St. Paul calls the *arabon*, the down payment of the Kingdom, the wedding of the bride and the bridegroom. The Church ceases to be God saving us by sharing his life with us. Instead the church becomes the organization for those who have been saved and are Bible-believing or those who believe in empowerment and liberation or those who are on a journey. Many parish churches are crucified and paralyzed by the competition and conflict between these kinds of groups in the parish as they struggle for a church "that fills my needs."

The confusion about the meaning of salvation is a huge problem afflicting the life of everyone in the church and seriously hampering the effectiveness of the church's mission. It is a problem that is especially corrosive to the life of the priest. The priest has a special ministry, a special service in the economy of God's salvation. If it is hard to know the meaning of salvation, then the servant does not know the purposes of the master and becomes unsure of what he or she is supposed to do. There are three primary forms under which the confusion about the nature of salvation appears. Salvation is confused with an idea or concept; salvation is confused with an experience or feeling; and salvation is confused with a program of social, psychological, or political liberation.

When one hears of the "Christian idea of God, Gospel values, the Christian idea of the afterlife," there is a danger that God's salvation in Christ is being reduced to a concept in the intellectual realm. Christianity becomes a way of thinking about God, humanity, human responsibility, and so forth. The sacraments begin to stand for ideas, concepts, values, rather than being a participation in a living reality. This approach is a natural temptation that arises from the need to study the faith in relation to the other great world religions and the popular secular creeds of the moment. The faith must be objectified to make this study possible. But the faith of the Apostles is not primarily a theory which is to be abstracted from the "Christian myth." The faith of the Apostles is a witness to the saving acts of God in the life, death, resurrection, ascension of Jesus Christ and the coming of His spirit. The salvation of God is not an idea, the Christian idea of God or the good life, to be compared and contrasted with other ideas. If salvation is reduced to a concept, it will simply dissolve and disappear in the solvent of pluralism. The priest is simply then the representative of one option among many for a private spirituality and will secretly be on the lookout for a better idea. Such a self-understanding cannot support the kind of sacrifice that the priesthood requires. I once read a book about religion in Japan after World War II entitled *The Rush Hour of the Gods*. There is a danger now of the priest being trampled in the rush hour of the gods.

The salvation of God is also not to be reduced without remainder to one event or one experience, for example, the experience of "being born again" or the experience of "baptized in the spirit." Then salvation becomes not God's gift renewed in us daily through our fellowship with God in the Body of Christ, but a possession that tempts us with self-righteousness and threatens to divide the church in a new way between haves and have-nots. In this scheme the priest will either be a have or a have-not. The power of his or her ministry will not be the inner mystery of the priesthood but a public claim to a particular experience. The power and dignity of the priesthood will be constantly gainsaid by individuals who claim a more authentic experience. This confusion of salvation with experience and emotion is a rather natural reaction to the desiccation of the soul that arises from the abstraction of the first position.

Salvation is also not to be confused with a social program or a political agenda. In our politics and social relations we must witness to the salvation of God but no program of social progress can be identified without remainder with God's salvation. I remember when I was a student at Boston College, the great Liberation theologian Gustavo Gutierrez lectured to us, saying, "Liberation is very important, perhaps I shall have to die for Liberation, but Liberation is not enough, even for me not enough and for you certainly not enough." When salvation is confused with liberation, the

The Power and Dignity of the Priesthood

priest becomes the agent of something which has not yet happened, which may or may not come to pass and which is marked with the moral ambiguity of all human enterprises. Again the priest is attempting to have a power whose source is not an inner secret, the mystery of sacramental priesthood, a particular role in God's sharing of himself through his Son in the power of his Spirit, but a public claim to the status of victim or righteous liberator. Again the church is divided into haves and have-nots; those who have the right social and political agenda and those who do not. The priest comes to stand for something that, though it echoes and reflects important ecclesial themes, is nevertheless of the world and not God's church. It is good that there be greater equality between men and women in the social and political realm but that is not the same thing as mutual subjection in Christ in whom there is no male or female. The political world of righteous victims and wicked oppressors is the problem to which the great democracy of sinners, the great democracy of the redeemed is the answer.

Salvation is not essentially an idea, or an isolated experience, or a program. Salvation is God redeeming and rescuing His people from sin and evil. Salvation consists of real events that have taken place: the coming of the Messiah, his death for us on the cross, his victory over death, his risen life poured out upon us in the coming of his Spirit. Salvation is the re-creation of human beings and human society and, St. Paul says, the whole creation, in Christ. Salvation is a new life, a different life from the life of the world. It is not an idea or a private experience or a program, it is a reality. The Church is the sacrament of this reality. This reality is to be accepted or rejected. To accept it is newness of life, life abundant, life everlasting. To accept this life is to accept the new reality of God's sharing of himself with us which is the secret of the life of the church. To reject this life is to be left defenseless in the face of sin and evil, to have no help against the enemy of our souls.

There is also confusion about the problem of universalism that undermines the missionary zeal of the church. The evangelical and renewal wing of the church has adopted the theology of the American frontier revival. People are sinners in the hand of an angry God, and unless they profess faith in Christ through a "personal decision," they will burn in hell. The majority of our people and clergy balk at the idea that friends, family members, and faithful adherents of other religions who are unconverted but yet good and decent will be damned at the last day. There is an understandable allergy to the presumption of knowing what God will do with any individual soul on the last day; this translates into a missionary reticence, an evangelical timidity that threatens to trivialize the church and its ministry. The problem as it is presented in the popular imagination of our church is a distraction. We cannot know the ultimate destiny of any individual soul. We may hope and pray that God will ultimately turn every rebel home. We must leave open the terrible possibility that God will allow some to rebel against his love forever. We should resist the temptation to become preoccupied with speculation about the ultimate consequences of God's plan of salvation, profound though the problem may be. Rather we should focus our imagination on the reality of our own struggle with sin and evil. The drama of salvation is not primarily a theoretical problem to be solved, the problem of the relationship between God's judgment and the pluralism of the world's religions. The drama of salvation is the drama of real men and women who are really threatened with a real evil and who must face a real death, with real guilt and estrangement. The drama of salvation is God's real sharing of his life, his grace, mercy, healing, forgiveness, his recreating love with these real people in a real history through the one who is really his Son and in the power of whose Spirit the church really lives.

The world we live in is still a world in which there is no human answer to the problem of sin and forgiveness, where death and the devil are still the enemy of our human nature, and where the new spiritualities and the great world religions offer people yet more paths of laborious ascent to God. The news of God's descent to humankind in its distress with a sacrificial saving love, with the reality of a new life, here and hereafter, is still water in the desert, still light in the darkness, and still life itself to those who are perishing. It is sad to watch the church constrain and devalue its mission because of a speculative universalism while people are sinking into evil and despair in front of our eyes. If the priesthood is to regain its power and dignity, the priest must have eyes to see both the peril in which our people live and the blessing of the church as the reality of the new life, the place where there is a constant transformation of human life in the power of the Spirit. When we are blind to these realities, we are blind to the holiness and sacredness of the church as the locus of God's saving activity, and we see the church as a merely institutional and organizational reality.

There are many symptoms of the displacement of the church as a theological reality, as something which is holy and therefore has a holy order, by the church as an organization. There is the vain hope that we will find the solution to the problem of the church and its ministry in reorganization, in better management, in training for leadership, in the right social psychological perspective, such as family systems theory. These are all good things and good in their place. All these things represent needed improvements in the life of the church and in the skills of clergy, but none of them are the long awaited messiah. It is no good to be more efficient and effective if we do not know the secret of our life together and the secret of our individual callings within that common life.

Perhaps the most common symptom of the ascendency of the church as organization is the almost exclusive use of political metaphors of power in our church. There is much talk of the balance of power between clergy and laity. The feeling here is that the clergy have too much power and the laity too little. The image is of a power pie. If you have power, you have taken it from someone. The more you have, the less I have. This is real. These are the kinds of dynamics addressed in the canons of the church. They are wise about this kind of power. Our canons and constitution recognize that power can be abused by each order of the church, clerical as well as lay. But there is another kind of power such that the more I have, the more you have. This power is mysterious, abundant, and fecund. It is the mystical power of Christ, the power of His Holy Spirit gifting the church in such a way that the whole body is built up. The nature of this power is to empower individuals with unique gifts for the furthering of God's plan of salvation. Israel was not weak because Moses was strong. Israel was weak when it rejected the ministry of Moses. The early churches were not weak because Paul was strong. The secret of his power was his ability to build them up in conformity to Christ.

The church is an organization and institution. These things are good and necessary but they have meaning and purpose only as they transcend and fulfill themselves as elements of the Body of Christ, as the fellowship of the Holy Spirit, as a foretaste of Christ's Kingdom. The incessant use of political metaphors and power analysis is confusing to the church and causes it to lose its consciousness of itself as a pneumatic reality—a fellowship whose inner secret is an abundant and supernatural power to have a life of love with each other and the Father that more and more conforms to the love the Father and Son share with each other in the unity of the Spirit.

In the church there are those who are called to a distinctive conformity to Christ in his vocation to reconcile all things to the Father in the unity of the Spirit. Jesus says to Peter, "Do you love me more than these? . . . Feed my sheep" (John 21:15). To such as these, Christ through the Spirit gives a unique power, an anointing. The priest is a distinctive and unique agent of the power of Christ in the church: the Christ who at the cost of his life gathers the lost sheep of Israel, the Risen Christ who breaks bread with the disciples, who bids them look for the Spirit to come upon them, and who sends them to proclaim peace to all the nations.

We are also confused about the necessarily sacrificial nature of the priesthood. Our democratic and egalitarian instincts rebel at the idea of what appears to be an elitism. Both clergy and laity are loath to admit the costliness of the priesthood. There is a fear of two classes of Christians, of making the clergy into super-Christians. There is an insistence by clergy and laity alike that priests be ordinary, that priests have no special status. This can be seen in the move toward a false familiarity between laity and clergy, the abandonment of clerical garb, that traditional symbol of a sacrificial and consecrated life. There is a sort of perverse desire to have a priesthood but one which is not to be revered, to have some sort of order in the church but one which is not holy.

But God works his salvation by giving unique vocations to unique individuals. When a bishop is consecrated, the witness of prophets, apostles, and martyrs is invoked. God lays claim to every life by making a special claim on particular lives. "The Spirit of the Lord is upon me, because He has anointed me to preach the gospel to the poor" (Luke 4:18). A life that is surrendered to such a call has a unique dignity and power (what the old writers called an indelible character) not because it is perfect, without human fault, but because it can no longer escape the terrible pressure of being a means God has determined to use to implement his plan of salvation. God's appeal of love to humanity through Jesus provokes guilt and hostility and rejection that are overcome by the suffering of sacrificial love. The vocation of the priest calls for a close identification with Jesus in his humiliation and rejection and his sacrifice of suffering love. The priest can be surrendered to this vocation. The priest can rebel. The priest cannot escape. This is costly, sacrificial. It is to be identified especially closely with Christ's longing for the lost sheep of Israel, with his weeping over Jerusalem, with his disappointment over Peter, with his suffering and humiliation, with his cry from the cross, "Father, forgive them for they know not what they do" (Luke 23:34), with his patience as he walks with them unrecognized, explaining everything in Moses and the prophets pertaining to the Messiah, with his joy as he breaks bread with them after the resurrection.

If because of a confused egalitarianism the priest refuses to identify with God's hierarchy of sacrifice and service, the priest will miss the power, dignity, and blessing of his or her special calling. If the laity refuse to revere the reality of such a call, such a unique sacrifice, if they prefer mere comradeship to a mother, a father, an elder, a presbyter in God, one through whom God makes his unremitting, terrible, yet tender appeal for fellowship with Him through his Son in the power of the Spirit, then God's desire to pour out his power upon his people is frustrated. When the people revere the special sacrifice that is the life of a priest, they do not diminish themselves; they claim their own dignity as a people who are ever redeemed by a costly and sacrificial love. When the people discount and are irreverent about holy orders (sometimes, sadly, with the collusion of a cynical priest), they demean themselves and lose their dignity, and cut themselves off from a mighty channel of the transforming love of God.

St. Paul says in 1 Cor 12:26 about the Body of Christ that when one member suffers, all suffer, and when one member flourishes, they all rejoice together. The solution to the problem of a lack of dignity and power in the ministry of the lay order implies a corresponding problem of a loss of dignity and power in the ordained. We cannot build up one part of the church by diminishing another part. The church finds itself in a new and challenging missionary context. To be effective in this context will require prudence about cultural sensitivity, leadership skills, organizational effectiveness, etc. But these things in themselves will not renew the power and dignity of the church, that power and dignity which are inherently attractive. To this end, priests must regain a consciousness of their dignity and power as a unique and indispensable vocation in the economy of salvation. This is an essential step for the church as it regains a consciousness of itself as God's communication of his life to his people, as the anticipation of the kingdom which is to come, as the reality of God's salvation.

8

What Have We Been Telling Ourselves about the Priesthood?

THIS PAPER IS A review of some key works on the theology of ministry, lay and ordained, in the Episcopal Church over the last thirty years or so. Ministry is a popular and widely discussed theme, and I wish not only to evaluate the discussion but also to examine the theological ethos in which it takes place, and to consider the impact of this ethos on its quality.

Elliot W. Eisner in his book *The Educational Imagination* proposed that all educational enterprises can be analyzed in terms of the explicit curriculum, the implicit curriculum, and the null curriculum.[1] All attempts to teach anything include an explicit subject matter and an implicit lesson that includes the unexamined presuppositions of the teacher and the style, ethos, and medium of the lesson—indeed, of the entire culture of the educational environment. Something is also being taught in regard to what is absent from the curriculum. Materialism is, for instance, implicit in the curricula of most subjects in many schools, and something is clearly being taught about the importance of art by its increasing absence in our schools. The implicit and the null curricula are powerful educational media because they are hidden. The explicit curriculum can be engaged critically, but it is easy to internalize the implicit curriculum quite unconsciously. The implicit and the null curricula act more like socialization and enculturation than instruction. Habits of mind are formed by the steady force of the educational environment. It is therefore important from time to time to audit the situation. We must try to make explicit what is taught by implication

1. Eisner, *The Educational Imagination*, 87.

What Have We Been Telling Ourselves about the Priesthood?

and what is taught by the absence of certain materials and viewpoints. My thesis in this paper is that discussion of the nature of the church and its lay and ordained ministry in the Episcopal Church over the last thirty years or so has created a kind of school, an educational environment composed of best-selling books, conference and retreat leaders, and official church-study commissions—that has been teaching and forming the mental habits of the people of this church by means of an explicit curriculum, an implicit curriculum, and a null curriculum. I want to look at two key figures that are particularly representative of this educational ethos and whose works reflect its development. Both were seminary deans: Urban T. Holmes III, whose untimely death cut short his tenure as dean of The School of Theology of The University of the South in Sewanee, Tennessee, and James C. Fenhagen, lately retired from General Theological Seminary in New York City.

Urban Holmes was a prolific and creative theologian. In a series of books beginning with *The Future Shape of Ministry* in 1971, he challenged both inherited understandings of the priesthood in the church and the currently popular responses to a widely acknowledged crisis in the ordained ministry.[2] Soon after the publication of *Future Shape*, he became dean at Sewanee. Certainly his books and his approach to the ordained ministry were powerfully formative for a whole generation of clergy who were students there, who read his books, or who attended one of the many clergy conferences that he led.

Holmes wrote at a time when traditional theological teaching was under explicit attack. The cultural revolution of the 1960s gave rise to "Death of God" theologies and to a serious crisis of confidence within the theological schools and the ordained ministry of the mainline churches. Many clergy were leaving the parish ministry for more "relevant" professions. The spectrum of theological conviction ran from an insipid religion of mental health and moral hygiene on one end to a strident neo-fundamentalism on the other, with little in the middle. The ordained ministry and parish life of the old-style mainline churches were widely perceived as lacking authenticity and power. Holmes captured the attention and imagination of a generation of clergy by diagnosing accurately the problem with the church and its ministry as the disappearance of a sense of transcendence. He was critical of attempts to solve this by the return to a precritical theology (which Holmes perceived in much of the renewal movement) or by an

2. Holmes, *The Future Shape of Ministry*.

uncritical embrace of secular, professional models. He insisted that there would be no recovery and renewal of the church and its ministry without a theological renewal that could undergird the mediation of a transcendent experience of God as the main task of the church.

I was a seminarian during this era, and I remember that there were earnest conversations about whether one "should" be ordained or not, whether ordination had any meaning, and whether it was not even in some way a betrayal of Christian vocation to be ordained. It was striking that, at the very moment when the notion of holy orders was being so profoundly questioned, a book appeared that argued that the ordained parish minister was the key to the present crisis. The problem, according to Holmes, was that the churches and the clergy themselves did not understand adequately the unique role and function of the parish priest. With great wit and sometimes biting sarcasm, he critiqued all of the then-popular solutions to the problem of parish ministry. In *Future Shape* there are chapters on "The Teahouse on Elm Street," "Stupor Aut Stupidi Mundi" (the wonder of the world or the stunned of the world), and "Instant Parsons and Prophets Without Portfolios." He perceived that the attempt to solve the crisis in ministry by cultivating an identity as a professional counselor or social-change agent, as noble and needed as these functions might be, was a flight from the spiritual crisis of the church and an avoidance of the main task of the ministry, which was to be a *pontifex* ("bridge builder") between humanity and God.

To effect this recovery of transcendence, Holmes used his wide reading in the social sciences, especially depth psychology and anthropology. One of his mentors was the anthropologist Victor Turner. His approach to the study of priesthood was inductive, not deductive. Using the tools of cultural anthropology, he studied priesthood as it was actually experienced by clergy and their parishioners, and he then read that experience against the ethnographic database. At a time when the ordained ministry was being conceived of primarily as another managerial profession within a class of helping professions, Holmes was able to argue convincingly on the basis of observation that contemporary people had the same expectations of their priests that primitive people did, and that the function of the priest in community was remarkably constant across time and culture. Holmes had no trouble saying that for most laity the ministry of the priest was central to their experience of religion. He made the shocking suggestion that the contemporary parish pastor could learn a lot by studying the role and function of the shaman. He proposed, on the basis of Carl Jung's psychology, that the symbol of the priest was deeply embedded in human consciousness, possibly in some way physiologically, and that the role of the priest was as much a constant of religion as creed, ritual, and community.

The problem with the priesthood for Holmes was that it had succumbed to the rationalism and secularism of modernity. Modem, secular culture with its emphasis on production and control had robbed the world of enchantment. The church and the priesthood had acquiesced in this disenchantment. This loss of transcendence was the source of the crisis of belief and spiritual experience in the contemporary church. What was primarily needed was not a more professional ministry or a more laicized church, although Holmes did critique the parishioner as passive consumer. What was needed was for priests to recover their vocation as ministers of transcendence for the parish community. This was not so much a matter of learned competences, though these had their place in Holmes's vision, but of a charismatic priesthood. Priests were persons who because of their personhood were capable of being living symbols of transcendence. The role of the priest was to be a "liminal" person (a person at the threshold), standing with one foot in the "action mode" of the production-oriented work-a-day world and one foot in the "receptive mode" in which "God speaks from across the fathomless ocean to our consciousness... called to symbolize what he on his own cannot even imagine: that inner word of God, providing humankind with the light to see God's intention for creation."[3]

Such a priest was not to be the tame milk-toast and weak-tea stereotype but a "creatively weird person" who was unconventional enough to catch sight of the sacred through the cracks in the mundane. The kind of person needed could risk moving out of the comforting but reductionist structures of the culture and venture into the "anti-structure," the "abyss," the place where prediction, control, and efficiency lose their meaning and where the individual comes face to face with death and meaninglessness, the place of chaos. In the antistructure, one encounters angels and demons, and there the Word of God is heard. Holmes thought the business of the priest was to be a practiced traveler in these realms, to be able to bring something of his or her experience of God to the congregation, and to enable the people to strike out on their own journey of discovery into the enchanted wilderness. One of Holmes's images was the priest as wagon master.[4]

---

3. Holmes, *The Priest in Community*, 34.
4. Holmes, *Ministry and Imagination*, 256.

By using the social sciences, Holmes mounted an effective protest against the rationalization and secularization of the priesthood based on bringing social-scientific models to an examination of ministry. He captured the attention of the theological community because he used contemporary tools to reaffirm the traditional function of the priest. He affirmed the importance of competency and professional ability, but he saw these competences as special faculties that could be added to a fundamentally charismatic priesthood.[5] Holmes was able to make a very rational and, within the context of an increasingly secularized world, very credible defense of the priesthood as essentially, at its core, mysterious and non-rational. He gave good reasons why the crisis in the ordained ministry could not be solved without a renewed appreciation of the non-rational element in religion, the mysterious transcendence of God, and men and women who were able to mediate that transcendence.

Though his vision was informed by the social sciences, Holmes argued explicitly for a theological renewal of the understanding of the church and the ordained ministry. He saw priest, community, and ritual as interdependent universal fundamentals of human religious experience. The role of the church, the local Christian community, was to be the *Ursacrament* of Christ, the *Urmensch,* and the role of the priest was to be the living symbol of the presence of Christ in the community.

Urban Holmes was a classically trained theologian who read patristic authors in the original Greek. He was deeply influenced by the transcendental Thomism of Karl Rahner, David Tracy, and Bernard Lonergan. Holmes's soteriology was organized around the theme of hominization. The drama of salvation was the drama of becoming fully human. In Christ, God revealed God's intention for being human; in his death and resurrection and the coming of the Holy Spirit, God unleashed a new power to become fully human. This full humanity included access to the dimension of transcendence, the life of prayer, worship, and spiritual discipline. Hominization also included a commitment to fight all that thwarted human development. This truly human life could only be realized in a truly human community. The church was called to be that community where the new life of Christ was made manifest in the world. The priest was to be in the community as the living symbol of the fullness of the life in Christ, nurturing both the life-giving qualities of the community and the community's opposition to

---

5. Holmes, *Future Shape*, 255.

What Have We Been Telling Ourselves about the Priesthood?

the death-dealing structures of this world, whether these structures were personal, social, or institutional.[6]

It is impossible in a survey like this to do more than touch upon a few of the guiding themes in Holmes's work. He was a brilliant and creative writer, weaving together an immense range of materials from classical theology and contemporary social sciences. A bibliography of Holmes's works in a recent doctoral thesis goes to nine pages.[7] Holmes himself was alert to the hidden dimensions of teaching about the life of faith. His inductive approach begins phenomenologically with the actual experience of the priest in community, a perspective that is missing (and therefore in the null curriculum) in considerations of priesthood that are purely historical or doctrinal. He was alert to the implicit curriculum, particularly as it played out in the life and ministry of the priest. He saw not only explicit teaching, preaching, and pastoral activity as a means of education and formation, but also the personal style and ethos of the priest. Holmes made us alert to what was taught by the priest's own affect and attitude in the face of death and chaos. Holmes's concern about what was taught about the reality of God by the priest's own spirituality led him to write an entire study, *Spirituality for Ministry*.[8] He challenged us to differentiate between the fundamental human role of the priest and the captivity to any particular cultural model.

If Holmes had done nothing more than insist, at a time when the priest was in danger of becoming little more than a junior member of the helping professions, that the business of pastoral priesthood was to be a bridge between humanity and God, he would deserve our thanks. It would require a much longer study than this to do justice to Holmes's explicit teaching on the nature of faith, the church, and the priesthood. In what follows, I want to consider only what is implied in this vision and what is left out, or, as Eisner would say, what is in the null curriculum.

In spite of Holmes's commitment to theology and his desire to provoke theological renewal, the implication of his three major books on ministry, *Future Shape*, *Priest in Community*, and *Ministry and Imagination*, is that theology is a precarious endeavor with limited trustworthiness. Holmes's mode of working was to start the discussion of a topic, such as ministerial priesthood, with a preliminary examination of the nature of religious experience, faith, and meaning-making. His approach to these

6. Holmes, *Ministry and Imagination*, 252,253.
7. Guthrie, *Sacral Power*.
8. Holmes, *Spirituality for Ministry*.

foundational topics is nicely expressed in the title of his doctoral thesis at Marquette University, *The Expression of the Ineffable*.[9] Religious meaning begins with an experience of the transcendent that is mediated through culturally dependent symbols. All meaning is socially constructed and is so context-sensitive that no two people live in exactly the same world.[10] The power of symbols is that they mediate this original experience. The dogmatic tradition is to be revered, but primarily as the record of the mediated religious experience of previous generations. The meaning and content of the dogmatic tradition is so dependent on its context in time and culture that it can only be retrieved, if at all, by considerable scholarly effort. If two individuals of the same time and place cannot be thought of as inhabiting the same world, evidently past ages are lost to all but those most skilled in intellectual archeology.

Holmes was a minimalist in terms of the objective truth-claims of doctrine and dogma, and his doctrine of revelation is very spare. For him, the primary locus of revelation is in the depths of the human psyche, in the feelings and imagination of the individual. He is aware of the danger of privatism, and he argues for the priority of the religious experience of the individual in community. Thus imagination and feelings, which are the locus of God's revelation, are formed by the ritual, symbols, and life of the community. Yet all doctrinal and dogmatic formulations, even individual testimonies, are inherently inadequate witnesses to an ineffable experience in the core of the individual.[11] God is primarily, for Holmes, "mystery," here used to mean an inherently inexpressible psychological experience. This is different from more traditional understandings of the nature of God. There is a shift here from a God who is characterized by revelation and by God's desire to make God's self known (but who is always more than we can know) to a God who is essentially unknowable, a view evidently corrosive of interest in or commitment to the doctrinal and dogmatic traditions of the church. Such an approach must turn people away from history and a serious consideration of the original witnesses because it implies that there is no such thing as a trustworthy and enduring self-revelation of God and hence no resting place for the restless human heart. By implication, what

---

9. Holmes, *The Expression of the Ineffable*.

10. See the quotation from Holmes's thesis on page 235 of Guthrie's *Sacral Power*. Guthrie identifies Holmes as what George Lindbeck would call an experiential-expressivist.

11. Holmes, *Ministry and Imagination*, 67. The whole chapter is the most complete exposition of Holmes's epistemology and doctrine of revelation.

What Have We Been Telling Ourselves about the Priesthood?

the church has to offer is not the truth about God and God's redeeming love but a possible pathway on the generic human spiritual journey. It should come as no surprise that many clergy formed in this theological ethos turn out to be more interested in reports of the experiences of other spiritual traditions than in the great Christian teachers of the past.

When Holmes engages in historical investigation, it is often to deconstruct a part of the received tradition. Locating an idea or concept in history locates it in a particular cultural milieu *whose time has passed*. Saint Thomas, for example, believed in a rational substantial soul. For Holmes, however, it is no longer plausible to believe in a rational substantial soul, or, at least, few "reputable" scholars do; therefore Thomas's ideas about priestly character are not really viable.[12] This kind of dismissiveness pervades Holmes's books. The result is to imply that theology is an entirely culture-dependent enterprise, one that must begin afresh in each generation. In this view the value of past theological formulations is that they show us how people of faith in previous generations struggled to be faithful to the Christian witness and to the times in which they lived. Theology is then not a cumulative science in the way that hard sciences or even the social sciences are; rather, it is a tentative, delicate, fragile attempt to make meaning out of primary religious experience. So the conclusions of theological investigation are conditional and suggestive compared to the robust, conclusive achievements of the sciences. When Holmes is speaking strictly theologically, the mood is often questioning and searching. He is at his most dogmatic when talking about the nature of symbols or the reality of the shaman as a fundamental of human religious experience. It is true that each of his books includes explicitly theological sections, but they are preceded by long and complex explorations into anthropology, ethnographic studies, depth psychology, and sociology. We are overwhelmed by the sheer volume of social-scientific information.[13] The inescapable conclusion from the implicit curriculum is that contemporary social sciences represent a source of knowledge and illumination that is far more trustworthy than ancient theological texts. There is, in Holmes's earlier work in particular, a

---

12. Holmes, *The Priest in Community*, 161.

13. Gerard S. Sloyan, reviewing Holmes's *Ministry and Imagination* in the journal *Worship*, said, "His biblical exegesis is good (except for some strange views about a corporate Jewish response to Jesus and Christianity); his *occasional* use of the classics is refreshing. The insights into symbol and symbolism in these pages are important. It is the quotations and references to sociologists, psychologists, and culture historians without end that pall." My emphasis.

naive confidence in science as an objective enterprise without ideological presuppositions. He never turns his cultural analysis loose on his own tools of investigation, and the result is to leave the impression that the conclusions of the social sciences can be true and dependable in a way that theological assertions never could be.

It is, after all, of the nature of the ineffable that it cannot be adequately expressed. The lesson learned from this implied curriculum is that, when a crisis arises about the meaning of foundational Christian symbols, the most dependable resource for its diagnosis and resolution will be found in the social sciences. A corollary would seem to be that, if there is a conflict between contemporary social-scientific analysis and traditional Christian teaching, the tradition is almost certainly in error. The tradition is so unlikely to be true and so likely to be yet another example of cultural blindness that it will be tempting to decide the issue without serious investigation. I suspect Holmes would have been irate had students articulated such conclusions. Holmes did not want to prioritize secular disciplines of investigation over theology; that was not his intention. It is an irony that such a theologically committed teacher, who explicitly argued for theological renewal, should in his implicit curriculum have imparted lessons making that renewal problematic.

Identifying the null curriculum is difficult. How does one recognize what is taught by virtue of what is omitted? Holmes is clear that his approach is inductive and phenomenological. He uses this approach in order to compensate for what he sees as a void in traditional treatments that were pure expositions of the Christian tradition and omitted lived experience. It would be unfair to say that dogmatic theology is completely absent from his texts. There are explicit discussions of traditional topics, like that of the priesthood in relation to the sacraments in the concluding chapter of *Priest in Community*. Yet, on the whole, dogmatic themes receive little coverage. When Holmes does discuss them, it reminds me of the reports of parish organizations at the annual parish meeting where a few high points are mentioned and the rest is filed by title. He knew the theology well, but he was excited by the new light he saw shed on it by his reading in the social sciences. While the themes of dogmatic theology were no doubt vital components of his own theological vision, in the pages of his books the few explicit treatments of dogmatic subjects, like the synopsis on hominization in the introduction of *Ministry and Imagination*, are like islands in a sea of talk about the antistructure, communitas, and "the ineffable mystery that speaks to us across the ocean of consciousness." As a result, dogmatic theology falls into the null curriculum. By virtue of its absence or near absence, the relevance of the doctrinal content of the Christian faith to the practice of parish ministry is compromised. Students are bound to learn that it is possible, even desirable, to speak about the meaning of ordained ministry without entering into a discussion of the relationship between, say, the doctrine of salvation and the meaning of the Eucharist at which the priest presides. Holmes's great contribution is to challenge the church and its ordained ministry to be mediators of transcendence. Yet he also teaches, to some degree explicitly but certainly implicitly and via his null curriculum, that this transcendence is mysterious and ineffable, and tied only by very thin threads to traditional doctrinal statements.

The historicity of the faith also tends to disappear in these expositions. Holmes's understanding of revelation as the mediation of an ineffable experience through culturally generated symbols tends to beg the question of historicity, of events such as the incarnation and the resurrection. The great Christian doctrines are certainly present, and Holmes is deeply committed to revising them so that they speak to his generation, but his discussions of incarnation, atonement, and resurrection are so couched in terms of their symbolic, cultural, and counter-cultural functions that one is left unsure whether or not they refer to anything that ever really happened. In what way is the resurrection a fact of history in a world in which no two people inhabit exactly the same reality? In such a vision of reality, can anything be said really to happen at all? Or are we not doomed merely to talk of my experience and your experience? The *objectivity* of the saving deeds of God, culminating in the life, death, and resurrection of the Lord, falls into the null curriculum. We are thus taught to speak primarily of our experience and not of what has happened or of what God has done.

Holmes was concerned that faith not become merely "spiritualized" and so lose its grounding, its connection with the earth and the ordinary lives of men and women. Yet to speak of the incarnation exclusively in terms of the "primordial representation of the self and the embodiment of God's love enabling our wholeness," and of the resurrection solely in terms of death and resurrection as "root metaphor," tends to obscure for Christians the claim that these things *happened*.[14] Because of what is taught by *not* being taught, there is a danger here that the symbols of faith will lose their grounding in history. If this happens, we lose the touchstone for our

---

14. Holmes, *The Priest in Community*, 24.

religious experience. The constant avoidance of questions of history implies that the historical witness is unreliable and that part of the task of theology is to finesse the question of history, but this is done without ever addressing the problem explicitly. There is a danger that religious symbols will be evaluated only for their effectiveness in mediating transcendence in this or that community, or for this or that person, and not also upon the basis of their relationship to anything that actually occurred. Part of what makes Christian symbols such as the incarnation and the resurrection transcendent is that they also have to do with things that really happened. If this is so, it is awesome, and we need to ask what those events mean.

The relationship between the priesthood and other orders of ministry also receives only minimal treatment in these books. It is especially noteworthy that a phenomenological approach that focuses on the relationship between the ordained parish leader and the local congregation is not designed to consider the role of the bishop within a diocese or the larger church. The bishop is also the minister with a special responsibility for the stewardship of apostolic doctrine and for stewarding the testimony of the original witnesses, as Saint John says, to "what was from the beginning, what we have heard, what we have seen with our eyes, what we have looked at and touched with our hands, concerning the word of life" (1 John 1:1, cf.1John 1:1-4). It can only be a source of mischief and confusion to imply that one can have a comprehensive discussion of the ministry of the parish priest without speaking of the relationship of priesthood to episcopacy and the diaconate. To be fair, Holmes was not trying to present a comprehensive treatment but was trying to enrich the discussion with his inductive approach. Nevertheless, Holmes's intentions are not the focus of this study, which is rather to see how certain attitudes and habits of thought are likely to be formed uncritically in an environment where Holmes's particular approach and style are in vogue.

Just before rereading Holmes's books, I gave a series of lectures in our parish rebutting John Shelby Spong's recent critique of credal Christianity.[15] I am struck by the similarity between Spong's theological method and that favored by Holmes. Spong stresses (overstresses, I think) the cultural dependence of all previous formulations of the faith. He proceeds on the basis of a minimalist doctrine of the revelation. For Spong, too, God is an ineffable mystery, and the history of Christian doctrine is the history of people trying to make sense of their encounter with that mystery. Traditional

---

15. John Shelby Spong, *Why Christianity Must Change or Die.*

What Have We Been Telling Ourselves about the Priesthood?

doctrine and dogma are by definition conditional and tentative and no longer speak to contemporary people. Traditional doctrinal understandings must be abandoned because of the conflict with the "proven" conclusions of ideologically untainted physical and social scientists. The resurrection of Jesus Christ as something that happened in history is explicitly denied. There is a great deal of talk about transcendence, but it is a transcendence bereft of doctrinal and historical content. Holmes would, I think, be quite appalled by Spong's theses, but Spong is in fact pushing to their logical conclusions themes that are implicit in Holmes's way of doing theology. An excessive suspicion of Christian tradition, an excessive confidence in the conclusions of contemporary social sciences, and a tendency to speak of God as ineffable mystery in isolation from doctrine and history seem to me to be widespread among clergy, and to be the enemies of a recovery of a sense of the living God and authentic Christian community. One of the problems is that for many clergy this posture toward the tradition is not a critically examined position but an uncritically assumed presupposition. Could it be that many clergy have learned lessons too well? Have these lessons—taught partly by intention but mostly by inattention—socialized clergy into a theological worldview that they have never considered critically? Spong's book is merely an extreme and alarming example of a particular attitude toward Christian tradition and the historicity of the faith, an attitude in which many clergy have been formed.

Holmes's books and presence have been a powerful influence at Sewanee and in the Episcopal Church. In the years since they were first published, other books and authors have also influenced the discussion of ordained ministry. Another dean who has made a major contribution to the discussion of both lay and ordained ministry is James C. Fenhagen, recently retired from General Theological Seminary. Fenhagen has also been a popular retreat leader and speaker over many years at clergy conferences. Before becoming dean at General, he administered a program in professional education at the Hartford Seminary Foundation. After his retirement from General, he became the executive director of the Cornerstone Project of the Episcopal Church Foundation. The Cornerstone Project was initiated at the request of the then-presiding bishop, Edmund Browning, to develop programs and materials for the strengthening of ordained leadership in the church. Fenhagen's and Holmes's careers overlap. Taken together, their work gives us a sense of how the discussion of ministry has evolved in the Episcopal Church over the course of a generation of leadership. Fenhagen shares many of Holmes's concerns, and each valued the other's work. Fenhagen shares with Holmes a concern for the role of spirituality in ministry. He recognizes that the attempt to develop ministry for lay or ordained people cannot be sustained apart from a serious cultivation of the spiritual life. He challenges laity and clergy to take time apart and learn that ministry grows out of solitude, of time spent alone with God.[16] He also picks up the theme of the interdependence of the priest and community and the enabling role of the priest that was part of Holmes's vision. Fenhagen has said a great deal about what is called "mutual ministry"; he literally "wrote the book", and is in no small way responsible for the term "enablement" becoming a watchword for the role of the parish priest in relationship to the ministry of the laity.[17] In *Ministry and Solitude,* Fenhagen speaks of an emerging new theology of the church "that understands the church not as a community gathered around a minister but a community of many ministries."[18] This phrase has become a shibboleth in recent discussions of church and ministry.[19]

These themes are gathered together with some shrewd observations on the present state of the church in Fenhagen's most recent book, *Ministry for a New Time,* which is part of a "once and future church" series published by the Alban Institute.[20] This book is a good place to sample the contemporary discussion of the relationship between lay and ordained ministry in the church today. The book opens with a description of the changing environment that all of society's institutions, business, government, and nonprofit alike, are facing, and the need for a new kind of leadership to fit the new context. As Fenhagen specifies the shape of this crisis of changing times for the church, he outlines the current religious scene. He perceives the resurgence of religion as a force in American public life. This resurgence is a source of both hope and concern. Fundamentalism is the leading form of this renewal of religion in American religious life. Quoting the sociologist of religion Robert Wuthnow about "the serious threat in the

16. Fenhagen, *Ministry and Solitude.* Fenhagen dedicated this book to Holmes.
17. Fenhagen, *Mutual Ministry,* 99.
18. Fenhagen, *Ministry and Solitude,* 140.
19. See, for example, Stewart C. Zabriskie, *Total Ministry: Reclaiming the Ministry of All God's People,* and also the essay by Roger White "Teachers and Evangelists for the Equipment of the Saints" in *On Being a Bishop,* 172. White words it, "a community in ministry, not a community gathered around a minister."
20. Fenhagen and Hahn, *Ministry for a New Time.* The Alban Institute is a nonprofit church consulting and educational organization.

What Have We Been Telling Ourselves about the Priesthood?

dark side of the fundamentalism that fuels the religious right," Fenhagen worries out loud about the divisiveness that characterizes so much religious life both between and within churches.[21] He challenges liberals to take the concerns of fundamentalists about an America that is seriously "spinning out of control" and to enter into sensitive dialogue aimed at moving beyond the present impasse, finding an "inclusive center" where religious people from different theological traditions can find a "new moral center." "The quest for a new moral center is the social agenda that lies at the heart of the church's mission now and in years to come."[22] Fenhagen laments the loss of the Episcopal Church's missionary and ecumenical focuses while it has become preoccupied with internal issues such as the ordination of women, prayerbook revision, and the debate about sexuality. He says that these issues are important, but we must let the Holy Spirit lead us beyond them. Quoting Diogenes Allen, he diagnoses the problem of the Episcopal Church as *acedia*, or despair: that state of sadness in the face of divine joy wherein the mind is stagnant and the flesh a burden. "We don't trust fully in the redemptive power of God to renew the church of Christ and the world as well. This is the Gospel message. In Christ the victory has been won. Through the power of his resurrection, Jesus Christ has overcome those powers that would destroy the world."[23]

According to Fenhagen, the church needs to recapture its confidence in the power of Christ so that it can re-engage with the culture with an energetic ministry of witness and good deeds. Clergy need to see themselves as leaders of this re-energized ministering community. This kind of leadership requires a new worldview, a new paradigm. Fenhagen describes six elements in this new paradigm: the kingdom of God in our midst; thinking globally, acting locally; the new laity; the centrality of the small-group experience; scriptural authority and interpretation; and leadership for a new paradigm.[24] Discussing the theme of "the Kingdom of God in our midst," he catalogs a list of social trends, including the developing concern to find an inclusive community that overcomes the divisions of race and class, a growing concern over the gap between rich and poor, a concern for the world's children, and a concern for the environment. All of these suggest that "undergirding the emerging paradigm is a theology of the kingdom of

21. Ibid., 2.
22. Ibid., 4.
23. Ibid., 5.
24. Ibid., 7.

God that we must grasp anew if we are to be faithful in our discipleship."[25] The work of the Holy Spirit in the world is calling the churches to a "kingdom vision that alone points us to the unity we seek."[26] Speaking of the resurrection, Fenhagen says, "The Kingdom of God has come, and through the ultimate working out of this victory in the world, the dominion of God will be fulfilled in human history."[27] The concern expressed here for the poor and needy and the stewardship of the environment is inspiring, and it is expressed in inspiring words. I am caught wondering, however, whether Fenhagen means that the kingdom will come at the end of history or in history by human hands. If the latter, he seems to be flirting with utopianism and Pelagianism. I will return to this question later in the paper.

In the section on the "new laity," Fenhagen recounts the explosion in the number of books on the ministry given to each person by virtue of their baptism, "books now numbering in the thousands."[28] Fenhagen sees that the balance of power in the church has shifted from clergy to laity as the laity have claimed their authority for ministry. This is to be celebrated. Clergy will need to develop new models of authority based on their role as agents of empowerment for the laity. Fenhagen is, however, also cautious and sober about the inconsistency in the discipline, commitment, and readiness for ministry among the laity. Shifting the balance of power from a confused clergy to an uncommitted and unprepared laity will simply be to exchange one set of problems for another.[29] The solution to this problem, according to Fenhagen, is a renewed emphasis on Christian education and formation. Small groups are an important medium for this kind of personal growth and development. They are widely accepted by Americans as a primary experience of the community that is often missing in contemporary life. The church should embrace the small-group movement. Fenhagen is worried that the small-group movement as it exists is not sufficiently mission-oriented. In adapting this modality, the church needs to challenge people who "think we are caring because we care for ourselves but ignore those in need in other areas of our life."[30]

---

25. Ibid., 8.
26. Ibid., 8.
27. Ibid., 8.
28. Ibid., 11.
29. Ibid., 11.
30. Ibid., 17.

What Have We Been Telling Ourselves about the Priesthood?

The task of Christian education and formation is made difficult by the tension over the interpretation of scripture. Fenhagen identifies the tension between a "text-based" approach to scripture and a "theme-based" approach. He believes the Holy Spirit is pushing us to a new paradigm of scripture that he describes, in a quotation from the evangelical scholar Eugene Peterson, as "nourishment for the praying imagination rather than fuel for apologetic argument."[31] To describe the kind of leadership that will be needed for this new paradigm, Fenhagen quotes Max Dupress quoting Justice Oliver Wendell Holmes, "I would not give a fig for the simplicity this side of complexity, but I would give my life for the simplicity on the other side of complexity." This, says Fenhagen, is the challenge before the church's leadership today.[32]

The book goes on to report some of the research findings of the Cornerstone Project on the state of Episcopal clergy. There are signs of strength but also signs of stress and role confusion. The reason for this role confusion is that there is a time lag between our theology of ordination and the actual practice of the parish priest. "Our theological traditions have stayed the same but the actual practice of ministry has changed radically."[33] There is a need for the clergy to see ordination as "empowerment for the life of the church."[34] Reporting the findings of the Cornerstone Project, Fenhagen finds that the clergy in the study are able to read and discuss theological papers on the priesthood but are unable to articulate a personal theology of ordination.[35] Fenhagen sees a need for clergy to recover their

---

31. Ibid., 18.
32. Ibid., 18.
33. Ibid., 45.
34. Ibid., 61.
35. I participated in a group commissioned by the Episcopal Church Foundation to debrief this finding. I questioned the assumptions behind the phrase "personal theology of ordination." It may have been hard for participants to complete the assignment (as it was for some of us who were priests in the debriefing group) because they believed in a public rather than a personal theology of ordination. I also suspect that clergy are reluctant to share reflections on their experience of the nonrational side of ordination that Holmes describes. To speak of such things is not theologically correct in the church just now, but this makes it feel dangerous to speak of how the theology of ordination touches one at the level of personal experience. My reflections on the Theology and Priesthood Project are in a companion paper, "The Power and Dignity of the Priesthood," also printed in this issue of *Sewanee Theological Review*. Reprinted by permission of the author and the publisher.

theological roots and rediscover theology as a practical discipline.[36] He finds the meaning of the sacramental nature of the priesthood as being a "living reminder" in the heart of the community of the story of faith in which each person's identity and the identity of the whole community is grounded in Christ. Thus the priest is both set apart and set within the community as the "keeper of the flame."[37] Although Fenhagen challenges the clergy to work continually to empower their people for mission and ministry, that activist and functional understanding of ordained ministry is balanced in his presentation by the need for the priest to understand that the heart of ordained ministry lies in what the priest is for the community of faith. "Therefore there will never be clarity about who does what until the priest is sufficiently rooted in a theology of ordination that is personally gripping enough to make it possible for him or her to discern what in the long term is important and what is not."[38]

This emerging new paradigm of church and ministry as described by Fenhagen demands fundamental changes in the structures of the Episcopal Church. Structure, says Fenhagen, should follow mission. We need to reconceive the structures of our church from parish to diocese and national church levels so that they more appropriately support the mission of the laity to exercise their ministry in the world. "We need to reinforce the teaching ministry of the bishop . . . and allow the bishop . . . to be a participant in the exploration as well as the interpreter of the tradition."[39] The symbolic power of the bishop needs to be reinvented as a "source of energy for mission," but this will involve enlarging our "crippling vision of the church."[40] Bishops need to focus on building "empowering structures" that connect them with clergy and congregations and empower the mission of the church.[41] Fenhagen ends his book with an analysis of the dynamics of change, a la Family Systems theory, and with a plea to make deep and systemic change, and to persist in the face of the resistance that is bound to come but which must be confronted in the interest of the renewal of the church and its ministry.

36. Fenhagen and Hahn, *Ministry for a New Time*, 52.
37. Ibid., 60.
38. Ibid., 58.
39. Ibid., 73.
40. Ibid., 73.
41. Ibid., 78.

What Have We Been Telling Ourselves about the Priesthood?

Fenhagen is a canny observer and cares passionately about the renewal of the church. The renewal of the ministry of all the baptized is one of the glories of the 1979 *Book of Common Prayer*, and Fenhagen does an admirable job of describing the changes and difficulties that incorporating this change has caused, as well as the promise for dynamic church life that still needs to be claimed. He calls for a renewed understanding of the interdependence of priest and people as well as for greater mutual support. He challenges the laity to bring to their newly empowered role in the church a commitment and dedication to growth in faith and spiritual life that is consistent with the dignity of their calling. He calls our attention to bureaucratic church structures that have outlived their usefulness and are not sanctioned by any theological vision. He makes the eminently sensible suggestion that structure should follow mission, a suggestion that will resonate with many of the faithful who have run obstacle courses for purposes no one can now remember. He addresses the tension between a functional understanding of ministry and a theological understanding of ministry. He asks the priest to be as attentive to the identity of priesthood as to its function. Fenhagen asks us to rethink the episcopacy and to reconnect a disconnected episcopacy with the clergy and the people and their congregations. He bids us renew the ancient and honorable teaching office of the bishop. He calls explicitly for theological renewal. If the church were to follow only one or two of his practical prescriptions, our situation would be vastly improved.

Fenhagen's book and others like it shape the discussion about lay and ordained ministry in the Episcopal Church in such a way as to create an educational environment in which church people are formed not only by explicit teaching with which they can critically engage, but also by having their patterns of thought formed by the habitual unexamined implications and assumptions of the discussion. To that end, I turn now to the way these books help express and form an implicit curriculum and a null curriculum in which seminarians, clergy, and laity are being (unwittingly) educated.

As I said earlier, I find Fenhagen's discussion of the kingdom of God disquieting. It begins to sound like a utopian project of works righteousness. I can only hope that he does not really mean that the kingdom will be established in history by human hands, but this seems to be what he implies. It is natural that clergy constantly exposed to such rhetoric will tend to preach and teach a semi-Pelagian religion of good works. Despite the many inspiring and appealing elements in the vision that Fenhagen outlines, it implies (as does much discussion in the church today) a church and ministry more indebted to congregational and sectarian impulses than to catholic and Anglican sensibilities. The sectarian impulse is to purify the church and create a fellowship of "true Christians." It is inevitable that a fellowship thus conceived will be reluctant to admit any source of authority outside itself. The vision of the church presented here is of a highly committed group of highly trained lay ministers who are energized by their clergy for service in the world. This, like all sectarian visions of the church, is very appealing. It takes the call of the church to holiness very seriously. Here holiness is not so much expressed in personal virtues but in committed action in the world. This kind of church is more a club for saints, even if sanctity is being given a contemporary activist accent, than a hospital for sinners. The Episcopal Church in particular is a lot better at being a church for the poor than a church of the poor; Fenhagen's vision may not necessarily shake us out of the arrogance of a suburban captivity. It may also tempt us, as sectarian visions do, to hypocrisy, to rest not in God's grace but in our own righteous accomplishments. The vision that Fenhagen presents is appealing, but it needs to be balanced by attention to other dimensions in the life of the church.

The work of Avery Dulles is helpful here.[42] Dulles argues that different ecclesiologies depend on different root metaphors. Each one of these metaphors gives rise to a different model of the church. He identifies five models of the church: institution, living body, sacrament, herald, and servant. Dulles maintains that since the different models represent different concerns and employ different images and vocabularies, a truly adequate ecclesiology will attempt to keep the insights of all the models in creative tension. Fenhagen's work, along with much contemporary discussion, represents a collapse of ecclesiology into one model, the model of the church as servant.

The contemporary discussion of the theology of baptism seems to have opted for a thoroughly congregational understanding of the relation between the community and holy orders. No one would deny that baptism imparts the fundamental Christian identity and that baptismal identity is prior to and foundational to all other ministries, including the ministry of holy orders. In making this case, ordination is seen as something expressive of and granted by the "ministering community."[43] This is true as

42. Dulles, *Models of the Church*.
43. See, for example, Stewart Zabriskie's description of his newly found understanding

What Have We Been Telling Ourselves about the Priesthood?

far as it goes, but is incomplete without the traditional catholic element of the bishop, and, by extension, other holy orders as living witnesses to the dependence of the whole body upon its Head. The sense of the ordained ministry as being representative not only of the church but of Christ and of the original witnesses, with a consecrated responsibility to that witness, is left out in these discussions, a loss of something that has been a strong part of the traditional Anglican understanding of orders. Michael Ramsey's magnificent study *The Gospel and the Catholic Church*,[44] though it was written more than fifty years ago, still provides a valuable resource. Discussion of ministry at the time that Ramsey wrote had settled into a stale debate between Anglo-Catholics, stressing the priority of the hierarchy as a means of grace established by the Lord, and evangelicals, stressing the priesthood of all believers and a purely functional understanding of orders. Ramsey's genius was to examine the evangelical significance of holy orders and episcopacy. He argued that the three-fold ministry—the canon of scripture, the liturgies of baptism and Eucharist, and the creeds—were all created by the Gospel and were together the marks and safeguards of the presence of the Gospel in the church as the one Body of Christ. Ramsey held that all these elements are naturally interdependent dimensions of the catholic faith, and that it is illegitimate to treat them as isolated realities. The episcopacy in relation to the other ordained ministries and to the whole people of God is a living witness to the dependence of the local community on the universal Church and the one Body of Christ, to the dependence of the local community on the historical realities of the coming of Jesus in the flesh and of his death and resurrection. It is these historical realities that gave rise to Apostles and, in their turn, the ordained ministers in apostolic succession, and also to the canon of scripture, to creeds, and to liturgy as the interdependent witnesses to the meaning of the death and resurrection of the Lord.

Present discussions of holy orders and ministry lack Ramsey's insight into the evangelical significance of ordained ministry, especially the episcopacy, and do not apprehend the interdependence of orders, canon, creeds,

of Episcopal ministry "as part of the ministering community on whose behalf I was acting." Zabriskie, *Total Ministry*, 75.

44. Ramsey, *The Gospel and the Catholic Church*. It is remarkable to take a tour through thirty years of pastoral theology and find no reference to this landmark study, which transcends the "which comes first, the hierarchy or the believers" impasse. The first edition of Ramsey's book was published in England by Longmans and Green in 1936.

and liturgy, and so tend to pit these elements against each other. Sacramental priesthood has no significance apart from the community of faith, but its relation to episcopacy and to the other elements of the catholic witness gives to it a significance that makes it more than merely an expression of the ministry of the local community. Holy orders express the dependence of the local community on the universal church, and, even more, on the death and resurrection of the Lord understood and interpreted by creeds and liturgies.

In view of Ramsey's insight, the shibboleth "not a community gathered around a minister but a ministering community" is unfortunate. While this expression is positive in its encouragement of the ministry of the baptized, it tends to diminish precisely that *evangelical* significance of the ordained ministry to which Ramsey called our attention. There is an evangelical significance to the reality of the community gathered around its ordained leaders. This structure is part of the proclamation of the Gospel, a sacramental expression of the origin of the community in the facts of the death and resurrection of its Lord. This catch phrase of "ministering community" also tends to obscure the incompleteness of the local community, of its need for and dependence on the one Body that transcends all local communities in both space and (it must be emphasized) time. This phrase also encourages us to behave as though "ministry" were something that could be pursued in isolation from a consideration of doctrine and history. A new appreciation of Ramsey's insights could moderate some of the contemporary talk of ministry and community that implies an understanding of the church that is difficult to distinguish from the description of any other voluntary society and its elected officers devoted to good works.

Reading these books in pastoral theology spanning a thirty-year period, I am struck by the constant sense of panic in them (except, of course, Ramsey) about the rapidity of change. The world is said to be changing very fast, so rapidly it is almost impossible to keep up with it. The church by implication must run, nay, gallop, to catch up. In all of these books there is a constant air of urgency and crisis that becomes the basis of a fundamental apologetic for a complete rethinking of our theological foundations and understanding of church and ministry. The implication is that anything that is not the newest and the latest is bound to be obsolete. The constant appeals for an entirely new theology of ordination and ministry imply that theology never produces enduring achievements. It can lead us to be dismissive of our tradition. There is a danger of implying that something is good in the development of theology and church practice just because it is new. This constant ringing of the alarm bell can form an uncritical habit of the mind that is prejudiced against the old in favor of the new, and to a kind of theological hysteria, a panicked, uncritical receptivity to the latest thing. I am reminded of a comment I heard in a lecture given by Family Systems theorist Rabbi Edwin Friedman (whom Fenhagen quotes approvingly) that the anxiety system is sometimes right but usually only by accident. Certainly the church needs to adapt its practical theology and its practices to its context, but is the situation as urgent and desperate as these books proclaim? Shall we really throw out the entire history of reflection on church and ministry? Has nothing been learned? Have we no binding conclusions? Did Hooker leave us no insights about holy orders that might guide us now? Are there in fact some places where what we need to do is cling doggedly to understandings that are precisely non-contemporaneous? These are at least issues that should be debated and not treated as though they were settled. There is a danger of being inadvertently intellectually dishonest and of forming a mindset that is dismissive of the tradition.

Urban Holmes made explicit references to classical theological texts, railed against theological illiteracy, and called for a theological renewal in the church and for a renewed theological understanding of the church and its ministers. I have argued that his implicit curriculum tended to overwhelm this explicit teaching. As the debate has moved along, the call for theological renewal has been a constant. Fenhagen spent much time in his book mulling over the results of the Cornerstone Project, which reported that clergy had great difficulty thinking of their ministry theologically, and that management, therapeutic, and (I would add now) secular rhetoric about leadership tended to predominate in their discussion of their ministry. Fenhagen also identifies a need for a renewal of theology as a practical discipline that informs life and ministry. Yet in these books there is little or no reference to classical theological texts or conclusions. Huge theological themes are given the briefest of treatment, and words like "kingdom" and "Holy Spirit" are used with the barest reference to their meaning in scripture and tradition. It is not fair, though, to criticize a man for writing the short and provocative books he was contracted to write; Fenhagen was not attempting a comprehensive pastoral theology. The fact remains, as we have gone forward in the course of church-wide reflection on the shape of the ministry, the conversation has become thin. Very small books with very suggestive titles but very brief theological foundations, and with almost no explicit reference to the tradition, have set the agenda and vocabulary for the discussion of momentous issues. There is a need for theological renewal in the understanding of church and ministry, and the clergy need to recover theology as part of their profession, of their work. It will be very hard for theological renewal to come when it is implied that theology consists in using words like "kingdom of God," "mission," and "resurrection," as though everyone knew what they meant, and as though one did not need careful biblical exegesis or a sustained engagement with the great Christian teachers of ages past in order to be faithful to the theological task. We have inadvertently been teaching our people that theology is not a serious business. We have been teaching our people that theology has no proper object, no proper method, and no trustworthy conclusions. In these books, theology is presented either as a Sisyphean attempt to express the ineffable or as an attempt to find "an inclusive moral center." It is not presented as disciplined, prayerful reflection through which God will make God's self known.

In Fenhagen's work, and to my ear in much contemporary discussion of church and ministry, the transcendent element that Holmes wished to recover is missing. A Kantian subordination of doctrine and worship to ethics is a pervasive presupposition and part of the implied curriculum in these books. Worship is important, spirituality is important, but primarily because they feed mission and ministry defined almost exclusively in terms of action for social justice. Of course, the church cannot abandon concern for the poor and for social justice without abandoning the Gospel, but the implication of much of our church talk about ministry is that the significance of the religious task is primarily if not exclusively "this worldly." In our contemporary discussion of "baptismal ministry" there is little evidence of the light of heaven shining in the life of the church. The sacramental life of the church as preparation for death, as readying us for heaven, has disappeared. The last things, death and judgment, heaven and hell, are in the null curriculum. There is a witness to the resurrection, but primarily as a power that can be drawn upon in the fight with evil, especially social evil. This is true enough, but we need also to hear the words of Paul, "If in this life only we have hope in Christ, we are of all men most miserable"(1Cor. 15:19). Baptism calls us to mission and ministry. It also calls us to be ready to leave this life "in the confidence of a certain faith, in the comfort of a religious and holy hope, in favor with you, our God."[45] The lesson implied by much contemporary discussion is that it is possible, even preferable, to speak of

---

45. *The Book of Common Prayer*, 504.

What Have We Been Telling Ourselves about the Priesthood?

church and ministry without referring to eternity. The lesson imparted by this hidden curriculum leaves clergy impaired for one of the central aspects of parish ministry, ministering in the face of grief and death.

There is an illuminating reference to this issue of the eclipse of heaven in much contemporary theology in Pope John Paul II's book, *Crossing the Threshold of Hope*.[46] The editor, Vittorio Messori, surveying the proliferation of official church documents, makes this comment and asks the pope this question: "And yet to some it has seemed that this very loquacious church is silent about what is most essential: eternal life. Your Holiness, do heaven, purgatory, and hell still exist? Why do many churchmen comment interminably upon topical issues, but hardly ever speak to us about eternity?"[47]

The pope gives a very thoughtful reply. He includes in his answer the immensity of suffering in war and genocide that this century has produced and the need to balance the excessively private eschatology of previous ages. He catalogs good reasons and bad why emphasis on the last things has slipped into the null curriculum. Then he says, "I understand the fears of which you are speaking. You are afraid that the fact that one no longer speaks of these things in evangelization, in catechesis, and in homilies represents a *threat to the basic greatness of man*. Indeed, we could ask ourselves if the Church would still be able to awaken heroism and produce saints without proclaiming this message. And I am not speaking of so much about the "great" saints, who are elevated to the honor of the altars, but of the 'everyday' saints, to use the term in the sense it has had from early Christian literature".[48]

In the first parish I served, I was once asked at a parish forum why clergy wore black. Before I could answer, one of the older men in the parish said, "I will tell you why. It is a reminder that we shall all die and that time is short for us, and we should take God up on his offer of forgiveness before it is too late. The black reminds us both of death and the free offer of eternity and says we should not hang back." This is a simple and beautiful way of expressing the witness of the priesthood to the presence of Christ in the face of judgment and death. To recall the ordained ministry to the work of equipping the baptized for discipleship is a great gain in our understanding of holy orders, but it should not be emphasized to the exclusion of the

---

46. John Paul II, *Crossing the Threshold of Hope*.
47. Ibid., 178.
48. Ibid., 180. Original emphasis.

ministry of absolution and blessing, and especially absolution and blessing in the face of death. The baptized are not always and only disciples about to embark on corporal acts of mercy. They are sometimes penitents in search of forgiveness, supplicants in search of healing, and mortals facing death. If these elements fall into the null curriculum, our strategy for priestly formation will be self-defeating.

Holmes's and Fenhagen's books have been helpful and creative responses to the task of rethinking the mission and ministry of the church and the relationship between its ordained and lay ministers. Holmes's work reminds us that the role of the priest in the community brings us into realms where we are dealing with the deep structures of human existence. He reminds us that we have to deal with things that are fundamentally resistant to endless rearrangement according to our rational schemes. He reminds us of the role of the priest as a mediator of mystery and transcendence. As the discussion of ministry has moved forward, Holmes's message of mutuality in ministry has been heard and developed by teachers like Fenhagen. Yet Holmes's warning against excessively rationalistic and functionalistic understandings of ordained ministry needs to be heard anew. Both Holmes and Fenhagen have argued for the significance of spiritual life and discipline for any ministry, lay or ordained, that is to be authentic, and we should be appreciative of that teaching. They have both called for theological renewal. Nevertheless, the *way* theology has been done in these books and in our church discussions leaves us with a very thin understanding of theology and with virtually *anti*-theological assumptions. The church's mission must be oriented toward this life *and* toward the life of the world to come. We still struggle with sin and look for the assurance of forgiveness. We still need to witness Christ's love in word and deed. We still need hope in the face of death and the grace to face life's difficulties. We still need to give thanks and to find blessing. We still need to hear the Gospel faithfully preached and to have the sacraments faithfully administered. This ministry is going on in many faithful congregations led by many faithful men and women in holy orders even while we struggle to discover the most fitting paradigms for ministry in our times. When we find those paradigms, still these fundamentals of the Gospel will remain at the heart of the ministry of the church and its ordained servants.

9

The Good Shepherd[1]

I HAVE BEEN A shepherd of both the four-legged and the two-legged sorts of sheep. My wife and I helped to support the ministry in the first parish I served in rural Maine by raising sheep. The ordinand has asked me to speak on the figure of the Good Shepherd. This figure of Jesus as shepherd, as pastor, is the oldest representation that we have: a picture in the Roman catacombs of a young shepherd with a lamb draped about His neck. The crucified Christ is the most widely shared representation of Jesus, and second to it and closely related to it is the figure of Jesus the Good Shepherd. Closely related because at once we think of the biblical Good Shepherd, we must think of the one who lays down His life for the sheep, who is irrevocably committed to the sheep and flees not when the wolf approaches, who is faithful even unto death. This utterly unique Shepherd who is also the Lamb that taketh away the sins of the world and who is truly our peace with God and with each other—who is truly Life, Life eternal—the life of the Resurrection and of the world to come.

The great Anglican theologian of the previous century Austin Farrer has a sermon on the priesthood entitled "Walking Sacraments."[2] I believe that ordination makes a person a walking sacrament. I teach that a sacrament has two dimensions. It has an objective dimension that has to do with God's action which always has the character of unmerited grace. A sacrament also has a subjective dimension — our response in faith, our

---

1. A sermon preached in the Chapel of Trinity School for Ministry for the ordination of William Starke to the Priesthood, Dec. 14, 2007.
2. Farrer, *Austin Farrer: Essential Sermons*, 101.

To Persevere in Love

apprehension of the unmerited grace in and through this objective and effectual sign.

In the time that I have been a priest there has been great ambivalence about the sacramental nature of the priesthood. Some of this ambivalence comes from a feeling that such an understanding runs counter to Reformation theology, but mostly it comes from a mistaken feeling that the relationship between lay ministry and ordained ministry is a zero-sum game and that the needed building up of a church of disciples and the ministry of the whole people of God can only come about through de-emphasizing the ordained ministry. Clericalism is a real problem, but is not solved by laicizing the clergy and clericalizing the laity. Lay ministry needs advocates but they are least likely to be found among those who can only imagine the ministry of the laity as some kind of para-clerical ministry.

I believe the ordained ministers of the church are walking sacraments. I believe in ordination as a spiritual fact of great moment. It is characteristic of our approach to the sacraments that there is a temptation to domesticate them and to dilute the signs, to soften the inherent offense of the Gospel. Baptismal immersion which speaks of death and life becomes a sprinkling, and Communion bread and wine become predictably packaged and portioned. So we rationalize away the significance of the sacraments. But the sacraments resist. The ordinand finds it not so easy to shake off the awesomeness of the sign, and people who have been instructed to not have too high a view of holy orders persist in acting as though they are entitled to look to their clergy for a glimpse of the Good Shepherd Himself. The people hope in the words of the priest to hear the Good Shepherd's voice, and hope to feel the pastoral touch of this Shepherd who is also the Lamb of God, and who feeds us with His very body and blood, and thereby offers us a new life with God and each other, the life of the Resurrection.

Let me say a few things about the nature of the shepherding which I perceive as I read the Bible through the lens of my experience with the four-legged sort of sheep.

Shepherding is hard work. There is no question of Bo Peep and her snowy white flock. Caring for actual sheep requires a great deal of stoop labor. It requires from the nomadic shepherds of Jesus' time and place miles of walking in hard places. It requires endurance and the kind of physical hardness that comes from strenuous labor over many years.

To be a shepherd also requires great judgment. Every day the shepherd does things, makes decisions, tends the flock in such a way that the

The Good Shepherd

sheep either live and thrive or falter and die. When I was a shepherd one of the things that took great care and skill was to keep the nutrition of the sheep steady. Sheep must eat the right amount of the right kinds of grass at the right times or they will die. When I was raising sheep we worried very much about something called overeating disease. If the sheep eat too little one day and too much the next day some of the bacteria which live in the gut of the sheep will reproduce to abnormal levels and produce toxins which cause death very quickly. The typical warning for this disease is large numbers of dead sheep. This problem was even more complex for the nomadic shepherds of the Bible. The shepherd must carefully plan the path and lead the way so that the sheep have neither too little nor too much grazing, and get to the water hole on time (as the old hymn puts it, Where streams of living water flow, my ransomed soul He leadeth). In addition to the problem of overeating disease, there are the problems of poison plants and of predators and robbers. There is also the problem of knowing the way or of losing the way. Shepherds count their mistakes, the miscalculations, the lapses of attention, their loss of resolve, with the bodies of dead sheep. The flock of a good shepherd thrives, matures, reproduces.

So when Jesus says I am the Good Shepherd, He is saying that He knows the way, that He can feed us, and we shall live and not die. He is saying that He will protect us from all enemies and will not abandon us even at the cost of His life. He is saying that He has died for us that we might have life indeed. To be ordained to pastoral ministry as a priest of the church is to be ordained to make present in the midst of the church in a unique and personal way the One who guides and feeds and will bring us safely to His Father. Among other things it requires strict attention to the spiritual food of the flock and a fierce commitment that they are fed on the Word of God and doctrines of the catholic creeds, and are warned not to gorge themselves on weeds and those poisonous plants which are the opinions of men masquerading as the truth of God.

Our salvation is a matter of sheep who are lost, who wander in the valley of the shadow of death, who are set about by wolves and robbers, who do not have good sense about what is food and what is poison, and who are in danger of perishing without a Good Shepherd. We are in danger of perishing without faithful priests and pastors who by the fidelity of their preaching and teaching feed us on the wholesome Word of God.

We also hear these words of Jesus, "I know each of my sheep by name" (John 10:3). It is an astonishing thing that Jesus says here. He is comparing himself to the great kings of Israel and to the greatest of them all, King David. There is no question of these kings knowing each subject by name. It is not humanly possible that they should, and inconceivable that they should want to know each subject by name. Even shepherds of the four-legged type of sheep can know their animals by name only if they have very few of them. The numbered ear tag which makes dependable identification of individual animals possible is one of the great inventions of civilization; before its invention the idea of picking out individuals in even modest sized flocks would have struck Jesus' hearers as preposterous. It is supernatural love that is being spoken of here: the astonishing seeking, searching, and sacrificing love of the savior for each one of the Father's lost children and His unquenchable desire to gather them into the fellowship of the Holy Spirit. The love of the Good Shepherd is not like the love of any earthly shepherd and certainly the anti-type of the typical attitude of the oriental king to his subjects.

Let us not sentimentalize this claim of Jesus. Of course a good pastor will want to know the people and so far as possible the names and their histories. Unless the congregation is very small and changes very little over time, there are real limits to the number of names and personal details the pastor can know. I don't like very much the practice which has grown up in some places of speaking the person's name as communion is distributed. Newcomers to the parish are bound to experience it as an in-group versus out-group sort of thing, which is the very opposite of the message we should be giving at the rail. Even in small parishes the clergy are bound to make embarrassing mistakes. In my view this practice is drawing attention to the human relationship with the pastor and away from the real significance of this saying by Jesus, which is that He alone is capable of calling us by the name we will have in eternity. The priest should know the people to the extent possible. Inhuman expectations on either side are not helpful. What is more important is that the people should know that the priest wants to preach and teach the words of the one Word of God in such a way that there they can hear the voice of the true Good Shepherd calling them each by name. Diligence and faithfulness in that task is far more important and a far greater testimony to the evangelical and pastoral love proper to the ministerial priesthood.

Some of the most physically demanding aspects of the labor of the shepherd require at the same time great patience and tenderness. One thing that makes a shepherd successful is the ability to midwife the birth of lambs,

The Good Shepherd

occasionally assisting in difficult births. But the real art is making sure that the newly birthed lambs eat—getting mother's milk within the first twenty-four hours is the difference between life and death for a lamb. Some lambs drink very easily and naturally on their own. Some are too weak to eat and they can be helped; a little milk can be forced upon them even if they will not eat themselves. The most difficult are those called stiff-necked lambs, who will not eat and are strong enough to struggle against the shepherd who attempts to bring them to the milk. These also can be helped, but only with sacrificial perseverance and the greatest patience. St. Augustine says that the clergy must hold the faithful to the bosom of the Church. And of course this whole life-saving work is a wet, bloody, and dirty business which requires getting on our knees. It has about it the humility of Christ, His getting dirty for our sake, His perseverance in love even unto the death of the Cross. Just so this is a ministry and a sacramental ministry of life, the life the Good Shepherd has come to bring us, and that abundantly.

Now we come to an awesome moment this night. It is an awesome moment when in marriage a man and woman promise themselves to each other 'til death do them part, and make this promise for Christ's sake. It is an awesome thing when a person after much training, preparation, and prayer, makes an irrevocable commitment to Christ in the service of His people, and promises to be faithful unto death. Here the shadow of the Cross falls and here the rays of the Resurrection begin to shine forth. Here as in Baptism there is a dying and rising with Christ, the putting away of an old life forever, and the entry into a new life, the life of a priest in God's Church, which is a 'til death do us part kind of life. Here God acts through the laying on of hands on behalf of His people and for the sake of a lost world.

It is no dis-service to the baptized that a man should commit himself irrevocably to the ministry of making the baptized life possible for given individuals in a given time and place and so be a walking sacrament of the Good Shepherd who calls each sheep by name and promises to lead them through the valley of the shadow of death and into green pastures.

William, here is my prayer for you and for those among us who are thinking of irrevocable promises we have made to God and which God has made to us.

I pray that you will be unashamed to confess Jesus Christ crucified and risen from the dead, and to give an account of the faith that is in you.

To Persevere in Love

I pray that you will be unashamed of the fact of your ordination—of the fact that you are the priest of Jesus Christ and a walking sacrament of the Good Shepherd.

I pray that God will give you the greatest possible congruence between your life and the persevering love of Christ calling and gathering, feeding and guiding home His people, of which your life is to be henceforth an effective sign.

I pray that you will respond in faith and faithfully to this thing God is doing in your ordination.

I pray that many will be touched with the Good Shepherd's sacrificial love through this effectual sign.

I pray these things in Christ's name, in the name of the One who said, "As the Father has sent me, even so I send you."

10

The Priesthood and Angelic Failure and Angelic Joy[1]

ST. MICHAEL AND ALL Angels, what a feast! Here is an example of how nothing can be more relevant and contemporary and effective for a parish like this with a strong tradition of catholic worship, than keeping the great feasts of the Christian year, Michaelmas among them.

In the twentieth century when I was in seminary and graduate school, voices in the church urged us to downplay the miraculous, the supernatural and otherworldly. If we wanted to reach contemporary people, we were told, we should stress the this-worldly aspects of the faith. The church listened to this counsel and we have gained much from a renewed emphasis on practical love of the neighbor. (An emphasis, it should be noted, that has never been absent in the life of this parish.) But as we enter the twenty-first century, some of the elements of the life of faith of which we were almost embarrassed, the mysterious, the miraculous, the supernatural elements, are just the things that twenty-first century people find most interesting. Twenty years ago, talk about angels in the church would have been dismissed as hopelessly antiquated and irrelevant. Now people in this century are longing to be "touched by an angel."

What, I have been wondering, do the angels themselves think of all this new-found attention? What would they say about it? If you will allow me an exercise of imagination, I believe they would say something like this:

1. A Sermon Preached at the Institution of The Rev. Dr. Charles Miller as Sixth Rector of The Church of the Transfiguration, New York City, on The Feast of St. Michael and All Angels, September 29, 2000.

To Persevere in Love

"We are spirits who dwell continually in the presence of God and have been ordained by God to bring you messages of his love and tokens of his healing. We are meant to guard and keep you from evil influence and call you to justice, mercy, and righteousness. We are to remind you of the life eternal and give you hope in the face of death. We are to intimate to you the glory of the worship in heaven and encourage you to join with us as you worship here on earth.

Long ago we found out that we could not really do what God had ordained for us to do. We found that human beings after the fall (that is, after humans forgot who God is and what it really means to be human. What it means to be human is to have a heart that is right toward God and right toward your brothers and sisters) have a kind of allergy to the things of God and that a full-fledged angelic manifestation leaves them terrified and doubting their senses. (We get very weary of saying 'Fear not.') Even worse, men and women who have received a message at the hands of an angel, believe and obey because they are impressed or frightened. This is a problem because we are under strict instructions to give our message of God's freely given love in such a way that the person receiving the message is truly free to choose to accept it or not. This means we often have to operate at low candle power. It is very hard to get it right. We either end up being too overwhelming or too subtle to be noticed. The problems go on and on, for when people do hear the message, they ignore it as being from and for angels and not for mere mortals, or they think they should try to become angels. It is really worse when they think they should try to become angels. First of all, the message is that men and women should become not angelic but more fully human; and second of all, it is impossible for a human being to become an angel, as impossible as for a cat to become a dog and as unnatural. So we end up with results that betray our mission and our heart's desire to serve the loving purposes of God for His creatures and children. We were at the end of our rope with all this until He decided to become one with you so that you could become one with Him.

The baby in the manger and later the man on the Cross bring you to your knees without scaring you out of your wits. You can even accept His resurrection, because He has shown you His hands and His side. You cannot shrug off the message and the challenge of a life of love as unrealistic because you know He was tempted in every way as you are and yet, did not sin. The best doctor is the one who knows exactly where and how it hurts, and the best helper is the one who walks beside you and knows what your shoes feel like. He can help you in ways we never could. Now you have a

The Priesthood and Angelic Failure and Angelic Joy

healer, helper, guide, and defender who will be with you always even to the end of the age. If He is in you and you are in Him, as He is, so you shall be. Your destiny is to be higher than us, and we will sing hosannas at your transfiguration and minister to you in eternity.

He has come and has done and is doing that which we were under a sacred obligation to do, and which we wanted above all else to do, and which we could not do. Until he should appear, our ordination was an ordination to failure. In redeeming you, He has redeemed us. Now we have a ministry that we can do and that we gladly do, which is to point to Him. That is our main work now, to point to Him."

So, we find ourselves at this Celebration of New Ministry on the Feast of Michael and All the Angels. As we come to ask God's blessing on priest and people as they commit themselves to each other and recommit themselves to God, and enter a new chapter of parish life together, the angel's song is in the air. What they say to us is very pertinent for the ministry of priest and people. Men and angels occupy different orders in God's creation and they should not be confused, but the ministry of the priest, that earthly messenger, shares this with the ministry of the angels, those heavenly messengers: it is an ordination to failure.

You have allowed me to give voice to the angels tonight; give me leave to give voice to the priesthood. This is what the form of the priestly life forces us to say:

"I have been ordained to pray without ceasing and to so dwell in the presence of God that I might continuously and unfailingly bring you messages of His love and tokens of His healing. I am ordained to guard the souls of those entrusted to my care and to guard the spirit (the Book of Revelation calls it the angel) of this congregation and to keep you individually and collectively from evil influence. I am to order our worship here so that it intimates the glory of the worship in heaven. I am ordained to call you to justice, mercy and righteousness. I am ordained to call you to repentance and pronounce absolution and blessing. I am to remind you of the life eternal and give you hope in the face of death.

I cannot do any of this. It is not humanly possible. It is not possible because of my frailty and inadequacy to the task, and it is not possible because of that allergy and resistance to the things of God which we all share. I can only fail to do that which I have been ordained to do, but I have promised, taken a sacred oath, to never stop trying. The more faithful and diligent the attempt, the deeper I must go into my poverty as a man and a priest, the more I must taste of the mystery of Angelic Failure, that failure which I share with the angels, to be obligated to bring a message, to want above all else to bring it and to be completely inadequate to the task until He shall appear. So the priesthood bids me taste the mystery of Angelic Failure and bids me die. And here there begins to appear a portion of that mystery into which angels long to look. The more I die, the more I am able to point to Him. The more, and this is different from the ministry of angels, the more I die, the more He makes His appeal through me. St. Paul says it this way, 'I carry about in my body the death of Christ, that the life of Christ might be made known in me as well. Therefore let no man contend with me'(2 Cor 4:10). The more I die, the more He is present to His people through my ministry, the more effective the sacramental sign of priesthood is in me, and the more I begin to know the mystery of Angelic Joy, the joy the angels have in seeing Him appear and do what they could not do, cannot do: touch, redeem, and transfigure people with the eternal Word of God's Love."

It is customary at times like this to give a charge to priest and people alike. To your priest I say, do not fear failure. Angelic Failure is the secret of your priesthood. May you plumb this secret and know the sadness and frustration of the angels that you may know their joy. May it be given to you here in this place that by your weakness and utter dependence on Him, the Word of God's Love is made real and present. May the angels' song of praise rise in your heart as you see Him do what you cannot.

To this people, this parish, I say, Here is a profoundly gifted, superbly competent, and personable man. He can do many things well. He can't do everything equally well. (He is a package deal like all the rest of us.) God means to use his gifts and talents, along with your gifts and talents, to be a blessing in this place. But there is a further blessing to be had, one in danger, threatened with eclipse, in our church, and one which I dare to challenge a catholic parish to seek, the blessing God intends for His church through the sacramental sign of the priesthood. For this to come to pass, you must allow your priest to be weak, broken-hearted, poor. You must allow him to be a disappointment and a failure. You must allow him to be empty-handed, to have nothing of his own, and thereby allow him more and more by his own weakness, by his own dying, by his own utter dependence on God, to bring you the One who alone is able to save, redeem, and transfigure us, Jesus Christ Our Lord, to whom be the honor and the glory now and forever, Amen.

11

The Priest, Conversion, and Social Justice

THE ROLE OF A parish priest is to so present the love of God made known to us in Jesus Christ the Lord that people's hearts become once again tender towards God and tender towards their brothers and sisters. A genuine concern for the poor has from the Book of Acts forward been one of the distinguishing marks of genuine Christian faith. More and more we recognize that we cannot be concerned for the poor as individuals without being also concerned about broader issues of social justice. How is the parish priest to facilitate this conversion to the poor and the cause of justice?

Charles Dickens in his famous story *A Christmas Carol* provides a helpful guide for the parish priest in the task of forming in the people of the parish a heart for the poor and the heart for justice. The central character of the story, Ebenezer Scrooge, is a very good symbol for the natural mentality of most middle class people, including me. However he may look from the outside, Scrooge sees himself as a paragon of virtue: hard-working, earnest, thrifty, practical, and realistic. He is relentless in his pursuit of classical middle-class virtues, and he feels justifiably proud of the disciplined life that he lives. In fact, his values are a bit more noble than those of many modern inhabitants of suburbia; indeed he would be morally shocked at the conspicuous consumption of essentially valueless items that is so much a part of our contemporary scene.

But Scrooge shares with most of us the conviction that we have worked hard for what we have; that many, including many so-called poor, did not work as hard; and that in the general scheme of things, we are more often abused and taken advantage of than treated fairly. It is ironic that for many of the most privileged of us, the most vivid experience of justice we have is

To Persevere in Love

our sense of the injustice of our own situation. It is a mistake to ask people who think they have already given too much to give more. It is a mistake to ask people who think of themselves as victims to think of themselves instead as victimizers. Rather than feeling enlightened, they will feel misunderstood and will quickly tune you out.

Dickens doesn't make this mistake with Scrooge. He begins in a different place and at the right moment. He knows that something dramatic must happen to break Scrooge's shell. An impassioned description of the suffering of others is not the first thing called for. Instead, first must come a vivid experience of his own mortality and a sense of judgment in the face of death.

Dickens begins his story of the conversion of Scrooge at a sensitive point. Death has come close to Scrooge. Scrooge, of course, takes it all in his relentlessly practical stride, and for seven years he suppresses this intimate knowledge. But Dickens finds a way to pierce this defense, to get to the fear and anxiety that are the natural part of any true intuition of the end of life.

The instrument Dickens uses is the vision of Marley's Ghost. Marley comes to Scrooge and reminds him that he too will die. He confronts Scrooge with a graphic representation of Marley's own hellish spiritual state and with a frank threat of misery beyond the grave. . . .

"I wear the chain I forged in life. . . . I made it link by link, and yard by yard; I girded it on of my own free will and of my own free will I wore it. . . Or would you know. . . The weight and length of the strong coil you bear yourself? It was full as heavy and as long as this, seven Christmas Eves ago. You have labored on it since. It is a ponderous chain!"[1]

The first guideline for educating the faithful about justice suggested by this story will be difficult to take to heart, and it may even seem to some a return to a more private and primitive religion. Nevertheless, Dickens' approach with Scrooge suggests that the conversion to concern for the poor and for justice does not start with the presentation of the case for renewed lifestyle. It starts instead with an attack on everything that protects us from the fact that we are going to die, an attack on all that insulates us from the terrible possibility that God may allow us the misery of rebelling against God's will forever. A preacher who protects himself or herself from this knowledge has little chance of communicating it to others.

To put the advice clearly: contemplate your own death; lead others to contemplate theirs. Know the hell you are in; lead others to recognize their own hell, and to ask the question, why should death alter this? People are

---

1. Dickens. *The Annotated Christmas Carol*, 78.

The Priest, Conversion, and Social Justice

unlikely to change directions as long as they believe their actions ultimately have no consequences for their own fate.

The functional universalism of a great deal of modern preaching and teaching undermines the demand for this radical conversion in favor of God's shalom. At some point, probably right at the beginning, it is necessary to point out the "bad news" to which the "Good News" is an answer. This is Dickens's advice, and it fits well with my own pastoral experience.

Dickens begins his story of the conversion of Scrooge by bringing death close, thus making an opening to the emotional and affective dimension of Scrooge's life, which Scrooge is normally able to keep safely sealed off. Having gotten his listener's attention, it would be tempting for Dickens to begin to make the case and to sketch out, as he could so masterfully do, the sufferings of the poor and deprived. Dickens is wiser than that. He knows something that took me a long time to learn. He knows that you cannot understand the suffering of others if you do not understand your own suffering, that you cannot feel the weight of others' hurt if you cannot feel your own hurt.

After Marley's Spirit departs, the first visitor to haunt Scrooge is the Ghost of his own past. This Ghost carefully leads Scrooge to those places in the man's past where his needs for love, justice, and kindness were frustrated because he had covered over his own wounded need with the hard armor of striving and self-sufficiency.

Under the influence of Marley's Ghost, Scrooge discovered his profound fear and anxiety in the face of death. With the "Ghost of Christmas Past," Scrooge discovers his own loneliness, hurt, and suffering. He develops an empathy for himself, a nostalgia for his past, and a sense of remorse. As Scrooge begins to repossess the world of feeling he abandoned so long ago, an indispensable foundation is being laid for the moral conversion to which he finally comes.

"'The school is not quite deserted,' said the Ghost. 'A solitary child, neglected by his friends, is left there still'. Scrooge said he knew it. And he sobbed. . . . Then, with the rapidity of transition very foreign to his usual character, he said, in pity for his former self, 'Poor boy!' and cried again."[2]

Immediately following this recovery of the poignancy of his own childhood, Scrooge has his first compassionate feeling since the beginning of the story: he feels remorse for missing the chance to befriend a young Christmas caroler who comes to his door. It is a small beginning and

2. Ibid., 93.

To Persevere in Love

pathetically myopic, given the misery that Scrooge has caused his family and his employee for years. It is also a long way yet from the serious contemplation of the individual's responsibility for the poor and for the evils of the social system. The Ghost smiles at all this, but unlike many fervent social activists, he says nothing and passes on, respecting this first tender feeling, the beginning of Scrooge's moral development.

Once when I was a farmer, I fell through a rotten hayloft floor and broke some ribs. I went to the doctor. He listened carefully and without hesitation touched me and found the place where it hurt. Initially, I was not sure of this doctor, though I wanted to trust him. But when he unerringly found the place where it hurt, I knew he could heal. I knew he knew his business.

The same skill is demanded of the priest and pastor. The authority to confront people with the part they play in the suffering of the masses will be granted to the teacher who can, with a gentle hand, cause people to feel again their own pain. Such exact knowledge of the anatomy of suffering begins with a profound self-knowledge.

The "Ghost of Christmas Past" not only leads Scrooge to the painful moments in his personal history, he also reminds Scrooge of the love and kindnesses he has experienced. Scrooge begins to get a sense of the bounty he has wasted. He feels the contrast between the love of his sister and the kindness of his former employer on the one hand and the way he treats his own family and workers on the other. A chink appears in Scrooge's philosophy of scarcity and self-sufficiency. Because he has unlocked the pain of Scrooge's past, the Spirit has also unlocked the truly consoling moments. The heart that can bear pain can feel joy and gratitude.

At this point in Scrooge's development (and ours), thanksgiving and hence Christianity are possible. It is time to preach and teach about the riches of God's love towards us. It is time to count blessings and realize the riches that we have and are offered daily by God through others. A tender heart and a growing sense of bounty make it possible to endure a round of deeper judgment.

Scrooge is thus brought carefully to the point where he can look upon his failure to give himself to the one chance for love that came into his life. He is able to see the moment when he sacrificed his own true life and that of his loved one to the idol of security. Through the agency of the Spirit, Scrooge's knowledge of the depth of his personal hell becomes intimate. Having been built up, Scrooge is able to find a place in his past where the road forked and to count the cost of the wrong choice. It is a devastating

The Priest, Conversion, and Social Justice

moment, but it causes repentance. Scrooge is heartily sorry for sins against those close to him. His sense of sorrow about social evil is still to come, but when it does it will be built upon this first knowledge.

Dickens has an uncanny sense of the limits and rhythms of self-disclosure. He gives Scrooge (and us) about as much as can be born at any one moment and then provides a space in which the dark knowledge can be digested. Theologically, judgment and grace always come together. Dickens understands this. As Scrooge becomes more capable of honest self-evaluation, he also becomes more capable of enjoying himself. "The Ghost of Christmas Past" sensitizes Scrooge and opens to him again the world of feeling by helping him recover moments of pain, loss, and tenderness in his childhood.

After this haunting, Scrooge is far more human and likable than the miserly figure we met at the beginning of the story. We begin to think there may be some hope for him, and for ourselves as well. But a new Spirit is required to move beyond this point—the Ghost of Christmas Present.

The "Ghost of Christmas Present" represents a robust and earthy enjoyment of life. He knows how to enjoy food and drink, how to celebrate, how to party. A spirit of enjoyment has been absent from Scrooge's grim and driven life. Preoccupied with his need for success, Scrooge has forgotten how to laugh and enjoy life. Dickens understands so well that concrete acts of love proceed out of the sense of the fullness and bounty of life. Scrooge needs to be strengthened by this Spirit before he can look at the darker realities Dickens would have him see.

In the same way, parties, potlucks, and moments of fun together in parish life are not distractions from the serious business of being religious. They are a reassertion of the goodness and value of creation in ways that subvert the relentless and soul-deadening practicality of lives given over completely to production and consumption. Moments of real celebration break down our sense of scarcity and deprivation, of being overworked and underappreciated; this sense is our best defense against the suffering of others. Rather than being celebratory, though, not a few contemporary liturgies have the character of moral nagging: "oh Lord, let us not forget...."

Let us not forget instead to enjoy the simple and wholesome pleasures of the good Earth and of our life together, and we might even feel we really have something to share. This is the lesson of "Christmas Present," and without it Scrooge goes no further.

Under the tutelage of this happy Spirit, Scrooge's moral sensitivity begins to widen. He learns a subtle lesson as he is led to see the happiness

To Persevere in Love

and gratefulness of people far less privileged than he. He sees people who are poor, lonely, and in hard circumstances finding a way to enjoy and savor their Christmas.

When the Ghost at last brings him into the Cratchit home, Scrooge is most affected by the dignity and simple pleasure of their feast. This realization of the goodness of life, even life lived in tightened circumstances, gives Scrooge the ability to see the shadows that fall on his employee and the man's family because of Scrooge's neglect.

Scrooge is becoming aware of possibilities in life beyond success and respectability. He is beginning to see that small things matter and that it will not cost him much to make a big difference in the life of at least this one family. Having experienced the remorse of knowing how he has hurt those close to him, Scrooge is given by this homely spirit an intimation of the joy and satisfaction he might get from helping those close at hand. Scrooge realizes that simple things can count. The spirit does not miss the chance to present Scrooge with individual and particular cases of need. Responding to these needs builds up in Scrooge the desire and capacity for concrete acts of charity. "Much they saw, and far they went, and many homes they visited, but always with a happy end. The Spirit stood beside sick beds, and they were cheerful; on foreign lands, and they were close at home; by struggling men, and they were patient in their greater hope; by poverty, and it was rich. In almshouse, hospital and jail . . . he left his blessing, and taught Scrooge his precepts."[3]

If our response to poverty is only and always at the level of charity, justice will be frustrated. But charity has its place. Sometimes it is important to be presented with a chance to take food across the street before being asked to take food downtown. Perhaps it is important to meet the hungry people downtown and have a chance to respond to them before being asked to understand the role of overconsumption in world poverty. Being presented with concrete opportunities both to give and receive help in small but noticeable ways can lead people to begin asking the hard questions about the systemic causes of suffering.

One of the happier developments in my own community recently is the movement to reestablish companion dioceses and companion congregational relationships with churches in the developing world. This encourages people-to-people contacts and exchanges. Those in this country who are involved in these programs are often very motivated by the chance to

---

3. Ibid., 139.

The Priest, Conversion, and Social Justice

take on particular concrete projects that can make a substantial difference to recipients in less developed countries. Often they are overwhelmed by the richness of the spiritual witness of the visitors from these new churches. Such contacts have the converting power that Scrooge experienced. As we begin to care about particular people in circumstances different from ours, and as we experience that they care about us, it becomes more possible to see the world from the perspective of others.

The Spirit has taught Scrooge about the richness of life in the possibilities of enjoying homely and simple things; he has given Scrooge some knowledge of the concrete charitable acts that lie close at hand and suggested even the joy Scrooge might receive from such good work. Now the Spirit presents Scrooge with the most terrible vision of the night. Scrooge thinks he see something odd beneath the Ghost's robe. The Spirit throws open his robe to reveal two children.

> They were a boy and girl. Yellow, meager, ragged, scowling, wolfish; but prostrate, too, in their humility. Where graceful youth should have filled their features out, and touched them with its freshest tints, a stale and shriveled hand, like that of age, had pinched, and twisted them, and pulled them into shreds. Where Angels might have sat enthroned, devils lurked and glared out menacing. No change, no degradation, no perversion of humanity, in any grade, through all the mysteries of wonderful creation, has monsters half so horrible and dread.
>
> "Spirit! are they yours?" Scrooge could say no more.
>
> "They are Man's," said the Spirit, looking down upon them. "And they cling to me, appealing from their fathers. This boy is Ignorance. This girl is Want. Beware them both, and all of their degree, but most of all beware this boy, for on his brow I see that written which is Doomed, unless the writing be erased." . . .
>
> "Have they no refuge or resource?" cried Scrooge.
>
> "Are there no prisons?" said the Spirit, turning on him for the last time with his own words, "Are there no workhouses?"[4]

Dickens by means of the Spirit of the Present causes Scrooge to look not upon particular cases, but upon the enormity of the suffering of the poor. He pushes him to face the tawdriness of conventional analyses and palliatives. Now Scrooge is strong enough to take it, though it is hard. The blindness of self-congratulation that was in his original perspective is completely broken. Scrooge is learning to see the world in a very different way,

4. Ibid., 142.

one that will push him toward a more thorough conversion. But the night is not yet over. There is one ghost left.

The Ghost of Christmas Future is the phantom of death. Once again, Scrooge is compelled to contemplate mortality. This Spirit shows Scrooge's death at the end of an unchanged life. In this vision, time has run out. It is too late. Nothing has changed, and the Ghost leads Scrooge to taste the baleful consequences. Scrooge is tortured by the fear that he will not have a chance to do the things he knows need doing if the vision is not to become his destiny.

"Good Spirit . . . Assure me that I yet may change these shadows you have shown me, by an altered life! . . . I will honor Christmas in my heart, and try to keep it all the year. I will live in the Past, the Present, and the Future. The Spirits of all Three shall strive within me. I will not shut out the lessons that they teach. Oh, tell me I may sponge away the writing on this stone!"[5]

The possibility that it may be too late torments Scrooge. Dickens' last piece of advice brings us back to the beginning—the anxiety over death. I do not see how the biblical sense of crisis and the need for decision, commitment, and action can be regained without our finding a way to speak of death and judgment. It would be a terrible irony to make into opposites the ministry preparing people for death and the ministry of promoting moral conversion. Each of these ministries is impossible without the other.

We know the ending of our story. Scrooge awakens and finds he does have time left and, unlike too many converts to the cause of social justice, he sets out with a heart full of thanksgiving to take advantage of the opportunities God places in his path.

What I most like about the story is that Scrooge becomes both more *just* and more *happy*. Scrooge's more responsible and caring life is also a more joyous life. The Spirits unlocked the place where painful memories, tender feelings, and thorough self-evaluation all grow together. Joy grows there too. People need to know that, also, and to see it, in us. "And it was always said of him, that he knew how to keep Christmas well, if any man alive possessed the knowledge. May that be truly said of us, and all of us! And so, as Tiny Tim observed, God Bless Us, Every One."[6]

---

5. Ibid., 160.
6. Ibid., 172.

12

What Do The Clergy Need to Know?

THE INVITATION TO REFLECT on this question causes me to be glad and grateful that I know some things and wish devoutly that I knew better some other things. I am very aware that what I have to say about this question has a great deal to do with my context in ministry. I was trained in seminary to provide pastoral care, liturgical leadership, preaching, and teaching (in about that order of significance) for a settled Christian people. I now find myself increasingly in a missionary context in a culture that is at once sophisticated and superstitious, and in which many people have never heard, or barely heard, or misheard, the fundamental Christian proclamation. The big thing that clergy need to know is that the calling is shifting to a more explicitly missionary, evangelical calling. I doubt that we need an utterly new seminary curriculum, but we do need to approach the seminary experience with a sharpened sense of the missionary shape of ordained service in the contemporary church.

Let me begin with what I am grateful for knowing. I am grateful for a sense of the supernatural and miraculous that I breathed in from the religious atmosphere of the church of my childhood. I have always known that there were learned, wise, and cultured people who had one foot in another, unseen, world. Although the sense of the supernatural is necessarily personal, the ethos of a seminary can facilitate and cultivate the spiritual sight which perceives the reality of the unseen world, or the ethos of a seminary can collude with the secularizing trend of the society. I grew up taught by monastics, hearing the Latin Mass, deeply formed by a mystical and sacramental view of reality. It has left me with a reverence for the Church, for the sacraments and for Holy Orders, which I count a great blessing. There is a kind of knowledge to be had here, which I got in childhood but that can be got in other ways, the lack of which seems to me a great hindrance for a priest.

I am grateful for a very traditional liberal arts education. My college (New College, Sarasota, Florida) was organized around a basic presentation of the history and development of Western thought and culture. There was an emphasis on the relationship between the leading ideas in philosophy, politics, and the arts, and the evolution and transformation of broad cultural trends. A great deal of emphasis was placed on the ability to analyze and articulate arguments. The seminar was the fundamental format for education. Being able to articulate an argument, civilly but rigorously, was the sign of accomplishment. Argument by assertion, ad hominem argument, and question begging were understood to be signs of a lack of accomplishment. I am especially grateful for practice in taking a critical posture toward theories and for being given some historical perspective on the history of theory-making. As a sometime teacher in seminaries, I find that many students have real difficulty taking a critical posture toward theory and ideology. The students are able and talented. They simply lack practice in this kind of second order thinking. Graduate theological education often assumes that students have a background and perspective which contemporary college courses do not necessarily provide. The story of how Western Civilization has gotten to its present impasse needs to be part of the equipment of the priest who is being called to be a missionary to that culture. A basic familiarization with the history of ideas and the nature of philosophy, including political and social philosophy, is very important. There is a need for a kind of liberal arts boot camp for those who have not had this basic exposure.

I am grateful for the biblical studies that I pursued in seminary. The historical-critical method is a powerful tool of interpretation and exposition and a part of the necessary equipment of a priest. This approach to the study of the Bible needs to be balanced by other approaches. The clergy especially need to have a sense of the narrative unity of the Bible. That the Bible tells a story that begins with Genesis and ends with Revelation, and that throughout it is one story of promise and fulfillment, one story of grace, is something that was not presented to me in seminary. Clergy need the balance of narrative and canonical approaches to scriptural study.

When I was in seminary it was popular to opt out of language studies. I took that option and regard it as the biggest educational mistake I have

What Do The Clergy Need to Know?

made. I have since made some remedial efforts. A priest needs to know enough Greek and enough Hebrew to understand the problem of translation and the part interpretation plays in any translation. The clergy need to be able to use an interlinear text and the grammars and lexicons and other aids to study in order to understand the choices made by the various English versions. The clergy need to have a small vocabulary of key Greek and Hebrew words like *messiah* and *eucharist*. Within a body of clergy, there needs to be a critical mass of clerics who are able with the original languages, but every cleric needs a familiarity with the languages of the Bible. As language skills fade, the temptation to be dishonest with the text is harder to resist. The fundamental task of preaching is a task of translation, of making the Word live in the present moment. The preacher treads a path somewhere between translation and paraphrase. For the most part, we start with a familiar but somewhat opaque English text and seek to bring it alive. It is very hard to do that without some sense of the moves that have already been made in the translation process. It is hard to perform the task of interpretation without some sense of how the Bible writers think, and that is hard to acquire without at least a familiarity with the original languages.

A priest needs to know how to preach. This is the place where the study of scripture and theology, self-examination, and the study of the people and times come together. Homiletics can be taught but the two main ingredients are exposure to great preaching and unrelenting practice in preaching. A priest needs to know that the kind of preaching most needed in most places in our church is simple, clear exposition of the good news of salvation in Jesus Christ. We need to realize that most people do not know what we are talking about and that we have to begin with first things.

When I was first ordained, the book that I referred to again and again was John MacQuarrie's systematic theology. It is not my favorite book now but it was the one theology book that I had from seminary that was organized according to the traditional chapters of the Christian story. Looking at the table of contents you could get some sense of how the doctrine of salvation related to the doctrine of the church and the sacraments. I think it would have been a surprise to the professors in the practical courses at seminary, but people in my first parish did indeed ask questions about the resurrection of the body and the real presence. This thematically organized book gave me a place to start in crafting my response to these very deeply felt questions. The clergy don't all have to be systematic theologians. Much of the academic theology that is written is simply too arcane, too wrapped up in professional disputes to be very helpful in the parish. A parish priest does need to know what is at stake in any presentation of the faith and how the chapters relate to each other: how, for example, if you get the atonement wrong you are going to have trouble with baptism and ministry, how your take on Christology will influence your preaching and pastoral care, and so forth.

One question is what clergy should know. Another question is what Anglican clergy or Episcopal priests should know. I think that Anglican clergy, including Episcopal priests, should know something about Anglican theology. One of the places you can learn something about what is at stake systematically in contested questions is in Patristics. The study of the Fathers has always been central to the Anglican ethos in Divinity. The world of the first five Christian centuries is more like our world than perhaps any other era in Christian history. There seem to be multiple reasons for spending a very significant portion of time with the Church Fathers.

An Anglican priest must understand the Reformation, and must have read at least some of Luther, Calvin, and the Anabaptists, and should also understand the peculiar take on Reformation issues represented in the Anglican Reformers and in the compilation of the Book of Common Prayer. A careful study of the Thirty-Nine Articles and the theological background of the 1549 Prayer Book would usefully organize many of these themes. There ought to be a chance to get in depth with some of the great Anglican Divines like Hooker, Donne, Herbert, and Maurice. The stories of how this strong tradition has renewed itself in the Evangelical and Anglo-Catholic revivals of the nineteenth century are things worth knowing in themselves, and for the light they shed on the problem of renewing the church in our own day. Michael Ramsey points out how interesting a figure Maurice is because he anticipates so many of the problems of modern theology in a distinctively Anglican way. It is curious that Maurice does not come up more often in the syllabi.

An Episcopal priest needs to know something about the history of the Episcopal Church. Parish clergy who are assigned to an established parish need to be able to interpret the story of their parish in the context of the story of the greater church and society. When I got to the parish I was surprised by how I missed having Greek and Hebrew. I was also surprised by how helpful history was and how often it provided the key to understanding parish problems and potentials.

What Do The Clergy Need to Know?

Spiritual formation is receiving some well-deserved attention these days. A priest should know the life of prayer from experience and have a knowledge of the depth and breadth of the church's ascetic tradition. I read many things in seminary that were opaque to me at the time, like the exercises of St. Ignatius, but which have become vital at particularly ripe moments later in life. The seminary course in Ascetic and Spiritual Theology should aim to provide an orientation and direction for further reading and study. It is important for clergy to know that in the life of prayer, one size does not fit all, and that different people at different times in their lives need differing approaches to the life of prayer, and that there exists profound received wisdom with regard to this problem.

There is always a tension in the seminary curriculum between what a priest should know in a general way and what a priest needs to know to be a competent practitioner of parish ministry. Some of the practical and prudential skill development should be seen as part of post-ordination training. A priest needs to know how liturgy and worship reflect and communicate a total sacramental vision of life and how the liturgy works in people's lives. I love C.S. Lewis' comment that most of the laity are more interested in whether something in the liturgy is meat or poison than in its original location on the menu. Alexander Schmemann also inveighed against what he called a merely archeological approach to liturgical studies. A parish priest does not need to be an expert in liturgical studies but a parish priest does need to have a liturgical consciousness and a liturgical conscience. A priest should know that when you are dealing with the liturgy you are dealing with the depths of the human heart. Proceed with reverence and caution.

A priest needs to have at least the rudiments of a pastoral psychology. Clergy need some way of conceptualizing the human heart, of understanding normal human growth and development, and of understanding how things can go wrong. It is important for the clergy to know that all psychological theories are a combination of clinical science and unexamined presuppositions about human nature and ultimate values. It is not possible to do theology without some philosophical framework, and it is not possible to engage in pastoral ministry without some psychological framework. The question is not whether you will have a psychological perspective but whether it will be critically held and consistent with your theology. I still find psychological perspectives coming out of the psychodynamic tradition of the depth psychologies the most helpful and heuristically powerful.

To Persevere in Love

Concepts like transference and counter-transference seem to me like necessary survival equipment. Family Systems Theory is a psychological perspective that has been powerful and helpful to many clergy and is now a standard part of the curriculum in many places. What clergy really need to know is not some particular theory but the difference between an idealized view of human reality, their own human reality and the reality of those they serve, and an honest and sober view of human reality, one which brings the hidden drama of the human heart into view. We tend to get this knowledge from psychologists; you could get it from novelists. Part of pastoral ministry is always the struggle to let go of how people should be and to find the grace to deal with them as they are. The clergy also need to know the difference between how they think they should be and how they really are.

I think the curriculum in the more professionally related subjects like Christian Education, Pastoral Counseling, Congregational Studies, and Parish Administration should be oriented toward giving students a sense that each of these areas represents a field of learning which has its own sophistication and its own standards of excellence. A priest should learn enough in seminary about these practicum areas to know how much there is to know and learn, and how well developed the thinking and learning in each one of these areas really is. In this missionary age, I am learning that I need to know something about marketing and management science. The dismissive attitude toward worldly knowledge that many clergy profess will not serve the church well. We need to know enough about many things to be able to bring the gifts and knowledge of others to bear upon the common mission. Knowing how much you don't know helps with this. The clergy need to know that their profession above all others involves a commitment to a life of learning and study. The best thing of all to know is how to learn.

13

The Priesthood and the Center[1]

WHAT IS THE CENTRAL task of the church? What is the central task of the church's ordained ministers?
 The official answers to these questions have varied little over centuries: to preach the gospel, to administer the sacraments, to pronounce blessing and pardon. In practice, in the time I have been an ordained servant of the church there have been at least three competitors for the answer to the question: "What should the clergy do and what should be their central occupation?"
 One model I would call the pastoral model. The church is seen as a community of healing, a place where people can come to find psychological and spiritual wholeness. In this model, the chief work of the clergy is to provide pastoral care. This pastoral care is often thought of in terms of one-to-one counseling, and the preparation and training are heavily therapeutic in orientation. The ideal pastor is sensitive, sympathetic, a skilled listener, non-judgmental, accepting, a good counselor.
 Another model is the prophetic model. Some of the seminaries of my denomination pride themselves on raising up and training a prophetic ministry. The central task of the church is seen as galvanizing Christian people to work together for a more just social order. The clergy are to empower

1. This sermon was originally given at a Scholarly Engagement with Anglican Doctrine conference at St. John's Church, Stamford CT, November 4, 2000, and subsequently published as "The Ministry and the Center" in the festschrift for Gabriel Fackre, *Story Lines*. The themes of the sermon are those that I have learned from the faithful teaching of Dr. Fackre. Reprinted by permission of the author and the publisher.

125

people to overturn oppressive social and political structures, and foster in their people "a liberative consciousness and praxis." The ideal prophet is courageous and forthright, able to speak truth to power, no people-pleaser, well-trained in social and political analysis, adept in the skills of community organizing.

Lately, a third kind of rhetoric about the church and its ordained servants has been heard, the rhetoric of leadership. Commissions on ministry and seminaries now signal that they are weary of the introverted and the non-judgmental and the prophetic bull in the parochial china shop, and are now looking for natural leaders who can be given advanced training in aligning the resources of the organization toward a visionary future. The church is seen as an effective provider in the marketplace of religious needs, and the pastor is seen as an effective leader, who can build a robust and dynamic institution with a shrewd combination of responsiveness to constituencies and the capacity to articulate compelling dreams of future success.

Most of us have been both the beneficiaries and the victims of these models of the Church and the work of its ordained ministers. The Church as a whole and many individual clergy have been generously blessed by the insights and challenges of each of these models. We have also paid a price. Many churches and many pastors have become exhausted trying to live out these models. There is an unreality behind these models, a problem greater than their tendency to overemphasize one dimension of the church's mission at the expense of other dimensions. Each one of these models causes the clergy to act as though something were true when it really is not, when something very like its opposite is actually the case. The best of people in such circumstances become very tired and dispirited, and some simply break down. The breakdown can be mental, moral, or spiritual. (We hear a great deal about such breakdowns in the clergy today. The reports are exaggerated, but it is true enough.)

What is the lie, the unreality? All of these models assume that the central problem is to figure out what the church should do. They all assume that the church exists and will continue to exist. The problem is how to take care of a settled Christian people, or to challenge a settled Christian people to action or to organizational effectiveness.

In the current circumstances, in which most of the Protestant congregations consist of fewer than one hundred souls at worship on Sunday morning, in which most congregations are on a plateau or declining in membership,

The Priesthood and the Center

in which the mainline churches stand at the end of two decades of membership free fall (the Episcopal Church has gone from about eight million members to fewer than two million members in this time), and when the median age of our congregations and clergy is fifty plus, it is unreal to take the existence of the church for granted and to take the continuing existence of the church for granted (at least in its present institutional form).

The truth is that we cannot take the continuing existence of the church for granted. Certainly we cannot take for granted the continuing existence of our denominations, nor, in many, many cases, the continuing existence of the very congregation we are serving. The question has changed from, "What should the church do and what activities should occupy its ministers?" to "How can there be a church here and now, and how can this church reconstitute itself with a new people in a new generation?"

What has always been the official agenda, the setting forth of Christ, proclamation of the Gospel, administration of the sacraments (in Cranmer's words, "to set forth thy true and lively Word and rightly and duly administer thy holy sacraments"), becomes the practical agenda in a new way and with a new urgency. The context has shifted. To a very great degree we do not serve a settled Christian people, but a profoundly unsettled Christian people within churches and an increasingly secularized, yet neo-pagan world, that for all its technological prowess, is more superstitious and idolatrous than the age of the Caesars.

We are confronted, both outside the churches and within, with people who have either never heard the Gospel or barely heard the Gospel or misheard the Gospel. To act, although with great skill and sincerity, in such a circumstance as though the existence of the church was secure and then to proceed to develop a pattern of ministry based on that assumption, is to be on a collision course with reality and to run the risk of spiritual shipwreck.

The central practical task of the church in our context, at this moment, is to tell the story of God's saving love made known to us in Jesus Christ, as though for the first time, to those who have never heard it, or barely heard it, or misheard it. (It is more difficult and complex a task, and one that requires greater persistence in the face of failure, to proclaim the Gospel to those who have barely heard it or misheard it.) There is a word for this: evangelism, even first evangelization. This is the central task of the church and its ordained ministers. Embracing this task allows us to acknowledge the reality of the mission upon which we have been sent, and the reality of the mission field to which we have been called. In this present

To Persevere in Love

time, that which was assumed must be made explicit. To tell a story for the first time calls for a kind of clarity and simplicity that unmasks any ignorance or lack of conviction hiding behind equivocation or finesse.

The central task now is to tell the story of salvation over and over, as though for the first time. I want to say what I believe are the central chapters in that story, but first I want to say something about the heart of the pastor and the end to which the story is told. There is a word, an Italian word, which helps me a great deal. It comes from the work of a famous teacher of children. This makes sense because work with children is one of the places where the problem of first evangelization, the first telling of the story, has been pursued with great discipline in those churches in which otherwise the missionary impulse is fading. Sofia Cavalletti, an Italian religious educator, says that the purpose of sharing religious materials with the child is to make possible by God's grace, *innamoramento*, the moment of falling in love with God. The central task of the church and its ordained ministers in this moment is to retell the story as though for the first time, the story of God's love made known to us in Jesus Christ, to those who have never heard it or barely heard it or misheard it, in such a way that this moment of *innamoramento* becomes possible, either for the first time, or becomes possible again. What is required of the one called to do this is not so much this or that particular set of skills or virtues, but this fundamental posture of adoration and worship, the posture of one who has personally known the moment of falling in love with God.

There is a great need now for the clergy of the church to re-center their sense of vocation and to refocus their efforts on Christian Basics, on a very fundamental presentation of the Gospel, on retelling the story, in many cases actually for the first time, and always as though for the first time, and in such a way as by God's grace to make possible this moment of falling in love with God. There is a need to re-center the ordained ministry of churches on what we have always said was the central task, even if our practice has belied it. There is also a need to recognize that the making of secondary things primary and primary things secondary has resulted in a loss of nerve, a loss of heart. There is a need for a new focus on things central, and a need for a new heart to tell the Story in a simple way, humbly and clearly, so that people may behold the fair beauty of the Lord and become lost in wonder, awe, and praise. This requires a heart that has itself been pierced by the beauty of the persevering sacrificial love made known to us in Jesus Christ.

The Priesthood and the Center

If our central role is to tell a story, the true story of God's persevering love for us and for all creation in such a way as to evoke love, gratitude and praise, then at the heart of our work must be a study of the Scriptures and the great teachers of the faith that leads us to a greater apprehension of God's revelation of himself to us in Jesus Christ. Our study must be serious, rigorous, and disciplined, but it must also be different from other intellectual and scholarly pursuits as it turns toward contemplation, and from contemplation toward adoration and devotion.

What is this story that we have to tell? It is the story of God's love. Of how God made us and all that is, and that God's plan for us was that we should have hearts which reach up to Him in praise, thanksgiving, and worship, and hearts which reach out to each other in love and service. Of how we were made to know God and to serve Him by loving and serving each other and cherishing God's good creation. Of how we listened to the tempter and fell into sin and evil. Of how our hearts became hard toward God, and hard toward each other. Of how since then, each one has gone astray and done what is right in his or her own eyes.

I must say something about sin before I move on in this story. There is a great dispute about this chapter of the story now, and there are even attempts to tell the story without this chapter. In the Bible, sin is hardness of heart. *Sklerocardia* is one word the Bible has for sin. Sins are actions that are outer and visible consequences of the primary problem, which is a heart condition. There is a dispute in our churches about which sins are the most important sins and about whether some things are really sins at all. This debate is a symptom of the seriousness of the problem of sin, our hardness of heart toward God and toward each other. One of the symptoms of sin is that it is hard to hear and to obey God's Word. There will always be things which we say we do, but which we are unwilling to say are sin, and things which we are willing to say are sin, but which we are unwilling to say we do. The reality of the sin which is absolutely beyond dispute is a crushing weight which every human heart knows, "the remembrance of them is grievous unto us, the burden of them is intolerable," as our prayer book says, and from which every human heart looks for deliverance.

Sin is an important part of the story, but in spite of some ways in which the story has been told, it is not the beginning of the story or the end of the story. We do not begin in sin and evil, and God does not leave us there. He sends His Son who comes in the fullness of time, after great preparation and at great cost, to make it possible that the word of the prophets might come true and that we might have new hearts: hearts of flesh, not *sklerocardia*, hearts of stone. He spreads out His arms of love on the hard wood of the cross so that the whole world might come within the reach of His saving embrace. By the price of the cross and the power of the resurrection and the gift of the Spirit, He makes it possible that we might have in us the heart that was in Him, the heart we were meant to have in the beginning, the heart that goes up to God and out to others. He has come to give His life for us that He may give His life to us; a life of worship, praise, sacrifice, and service, a life which begins now and which the grave cannot hold.

There is an icon that has great meaning for me, and helps me to focus on what is central to the vocation of the ordained. It is an image that is outside the ethos and aesthetic of the Protestant world. It is the icon of the sacred heart of Jesus. It is an image that has fascinated and horrified me most of my life. I remember seeing as a child the image of a heart, sometimes pierced, sometimes encircled with a crown of thorns, sometimes with a flame over it. It was mysterious and confusing. It is a common image in Roman churches. I was startled when I came to this church and noticed this same heart in the floor mosaic here, literally under our feet. It is part of a design representing the theological virtues of faith, hope, and love. Love, of course, abides forever. This heart doesn't have the thorns or the sword. It does have the flame, but as a radiating circle. It is an inflamed heart. Though the design is a little different, it is, nonetheless, the same heart I have been seeing all these years, the sacred heart of Jesus. If you look carefully in our churches and are alert to all the different variations the design can take, you will be surprised at how common it actually is.

The meaning of this icon was brought home to me when one of the saints of our parish died. Arthur Cassell was a distinguished Liberian diplomat. He was the ambassador of Liberia to the United Nations. His life was tragically turned upside down by a coup in his country, and he lived out his exile in this parish. He was a person of deep faith. His father had been the Dean of the Cathedral in Monrovia. Arthur was one of those people who befriend and encourage the clergy. When he died, his wife told me that Arthur had left something for me, something he got on a diplomatic trip to Iran. I could see it was a rug. I thought it was perhaps a Muslim prayer rug. It was, instead, a tapestry in very vivid colors and a very dramatic, even melodramatic, style of Jesus. It was something that was about as far from the restrained and dignified aesthetic of Anglicanism as you can get. Jesus is pointing his finger at me, at you, and looking out with large searching eyes, and with his other hand he is pulling aside his robes, revealing and pointing to his heart, inflamed, circled with the hard thorns of our resistance, but radiating love, this heart, the one heart God has ever meant for you and for me to have, the sacred heart of Jesus, this heart which goes up to the Father and out to us. And Jesus is saying, "I have come that you may have this heart. I send you to give this heart to others." Make it so. Amen.

14

On Being a Priest in a Difficult Time[1]

A Response to Reflections by Philip Turner and Christopher Seitz

IN MY NECK OF the ecclesiastical woods there is a standard format for sermons at ordinations, celebrations of new ministry, and Holy Week meditations on the renewal of priestly vows. The speaker is obliged to give a passing nod to the event at hand and then devote the rest of the agenda to a discussion of the preeminence of baptismal ministry. The hoary bogie man of clericalism is trotted out and denounced to the satisfaction of all present. Patriarchalism, hierarchy, are said to be bad, and collaboration and mutuality are said to be good. Something is often said about the ministry belonging to the people, not to the priest, and about looking to the members of the congregation who are the "real" ministers.

Like so much of the semi-official rhetoric in the Episcopal Church today, the problem is not the text but the subtext. The dignity of baptismal ministry, the dangers of clericalism, the role of the ordained as servants of the servants of God, who can deny the significance of these themes? (Though even these themes can be used in disturbingly hostile ways. I once listened to what seemed like a tome on lay ministry at the service to honor a

---

1. This paper was originally a response on my blog leanderharding.com/blog on January 7, 2005, to a series sponsored by the Anglican Communion Institute. The original articles are no longer available online.

On Being a Priest in a Difficult Time

priest who was retiring, beloved by the congregation, after a long and honorable ministry, of which 25 years were spent in the parish where the service was being held. While there was nothing wrong with what the bishop was saying, the context made it seem an astonishing indifference to a life of sacrifice and caused one to wonder if an intentional insult were being offered.) Very often these sermons and speeches about "mutual ministry" and "common total ministry" that are offered on occasions when the liturgy is speaking of the unique offering of the priestly life say little with which I would want to take issue. It is the subtext which often leaves me oppressed in the spirit. The subtext says in effect, "Let us not be confused. There is nothing happening here which has any eternal or supernatural significance. For after all neither the church, nor its preaching, nor its sacraments, nor its orders of ministers are really necessary in any meaningful way. Let us not expect very much of this priest. Let us not expect anything sacramental. Let us not expect any unique presence of Christ in the church through this offering. Let us especially not expect any unique sacrifice on the part of this individual. For we all know that if we require a profound and irrevocable sacrifice on the part of our priests we shall be expected to make profound and irrevocable sacrifices ourselves. And let us not be confused about the solemnity of this person binding himself or herself to the profession of the Apostolic Faith. Let us not think that anything dangerous is happening when a man or woman signs on the dotted line that they believe the scriptures to contain all things necessary to salvation or when they undertake to lead the congregation in the recitation of the creeds of the church. For if we thought that, then we would be bound by something more than our own unformed and uninformed consciences and would be obliged toward a dangerous and risky profession of faith ourselves."

Sadly sometimes one looks over and sees the ordinand happily nodding through it all, relieved to be let off the hook at the last minute. So instead of confession in all its meanings and a sacrifice of thanksgiving, we get one more ritual where we assure ourselves that our sins are benign and God is indulgent.

To cultivate a clergy who are encouraged as a matter of principle not to believe in the uniqueness of their vocation is yet another symptom of the difficult times to which Turner and Seitz's talks are addressed. Against the backdrop of predictably anticlerical and psuedo-egalitarian talk about the priesthood, this collection of sermons and meditations by two faithful scholar-priests comes as the shelter of a mighty rock within a weary land.

To Persevere in Love

Both Philip Turner and Christopher Seitz give very sober estimates of the theological crisis of the Episcopal Church. Both counsel perseverance and warn against schism and the sectarian impulse. Philip Turner takes up a theme that has become a hallmark with him, that is what is needed in this church that is embracing revisionist theologies and practices that are nothing short of apostate, is not more argument but more faithful practice. He argues that sound theological discernment requires a community of faithful practice. He warns us away from fruitless partisan wrangling and politicking, and calls us to renew the practices of prayer, scripture reading, and community life that might create an environment in which faithful theological discernment might take place. Turner questions whether the witness of scripture and the wisdom of the tradition can be apprehended in churches where the fundamental Christian practices have atrophied. He urges the clergy to pick up that particular aspect of their vocation which calls them to constitute themselves as a college of presbyters who meet in prayer, and particularly the scripture-soaked prayer of the daily offices, and in the context of this prayer, and with a commitment to the mutual charity and submission of true Christian community, take up the great issues that divide the church. Turner has faith that more people are converted by holiness of life than by argument.

It is a very odd fact of life in our church that the typical life of a diocese provides for little interaction between the clergy and virtually no connection between the bishop and clergy apart from official visitation. The vision that Philip Turner proposes of the bishop and the college of presbyters as a real Christian community gathered regularly in common prayer, worship, and spiritual conversation is hopeful. It is the monastic strategy for dealing with the unfaithfulness of the church. The monastic strategy seeks to renew the church by forming exemplary Christian communities while at the same time resisting the sectarian temptation to schism and separation. The proposal is to reform the church by creating within its structures islands of winning and winsome faithfulness.

There will be places where such a strategy will work and where community can even be built across lines of division. There will be other places where the polarization is too well defined and such community building is only possible among the like-minded. I endorse the effort. It will bless us in any event to return to the practices of prayer and study which should have defined our lives all along. But while we are praying and engaging in

On Being a Priest in a Difficult Time

the overdue business of renewing our Christian and priestly practice, the General Convention will likely vote us into new regions of apostasy.

I miss in both sets of talks a consideration of the priest, in the phrase of Austin Farrer, as a "walking sacrament." One of the things that have devitalized the sign of priesthood in our church is the way in which the bonds between the signifier and the signified have been loosed. To be a priest is to be someone whose hands are tied. While Anglo-Catholic ritual is not always good theology, it is ever good psychology, and the ritual of binding together the new priest's hands and placing in them the Bible and the communion vessels shows to all and no less to the new priest that this is a life that is by choice constrained by vow, by a faithfulness that allows no second thoughts. Thus, the people when they see a priest should know what this person is bound to confess and perform. We have already entered into a time which shall soon become more well defined when it will seem that we are tied to things which cannot be found in the scriptures, the creeds or the historic liturgies. Of what shall we then be walking signs?

Turner's proposals give us a spiritually challenging way to live and renew our vocation in a church which has itself become a broken sign, but a practical way of saying, "I intend to be a sign of this and not this" is needed. There is a need for some distinction and separation that is not schism and sectarianism and the fruitless search for the pure church. There is a need for clarifying the sign so that the sacrament may be preserved. The model of Roman Catholic clerical congregations is well worth considering. This has traditionally been seen in Anglicanism primarily in catholic circles, but perhaps the time is ripe for an order of priests founded on adherence to orthodox doctrine and commitment to practices of prayer, Bible reading, and study that could include priests from across a spectrum of churchmanship. It could give a way for the pastoral fruitfulness of different theological postures and different visions of priestly fidelity to be put to the test. It could give congregations a chance to understand easily to what sort of things particular priests are bound and for which they stand.

Chris Seitz's meditations helpfully direct us to the Old Testament. Here we find the story of a church more like our own than the church of Acts. He directs us to those prophets who are called to minister to a church that is manifestly unfaithful and corrupt. He reminds us that hidden within the prophets' words of judgment are words of grace, and that hidden within the words of grace are words of judgment. These realities are not mutually exclusive but hang together in God's faithful love for His church and are two parts of God's one act of providential testing and refining. It is very helpful to be reminded that in the Bible, the language of judgment is a language of purification and hope. The present chaos is forcing clarification, forcing decision, and forcing alliances that would have seemed impossible a short while ago. We must be cautious about identifying ourselves with the prophets, because prophecy is not a self-chosen vocation, but it may come at any time to any one of us. We can all be encouraged by remembering that the prophets were not in control of the response to their message or the consequences of the response. The prophets had a role that was given to them that required faithfulness and trust in the wisdom of God.

Providence is one of the great neglected themes in contemporary theology even in more traditionalist circles. It is good to be reminded that the Bible teaches that "man meant it for ill but God meant it for good." It is good to be reminded that the living through of God's providential history may well be hard. But that does not mean that we live in a godforsaken world. It is not beyond the powers of God to turn the present troubles to great good for His church. This should give us courage to persevere in faithfulness to our vocation.

I am also grateful to Seitz for bringing our attention to the role of the priest as intercessor. It is very helpful to do this by way of contemplation of the prophets. Thus we can put aside any lingering nervousness about crude and superstitious ideas of intercession associated with chantry masses and Reformation debates. We can see the connection between being the bearer of the Word of God and the necessity, the inevitability of intercession. How can the heart of the priest not be broken by the response of the people to the Word of God, whether it is a response of repentance or a response of resistance? It would take a very stony heart to resist the call to offer up prayers on behalf of these people, impossible once commissioned to bear the Word of God to a particular people not to constantly carry them on your heart as you stand before the Lord.

For me there is a disconnect between these earnest discussions that we church professionals have amongst ourselves and the reality of the parish and the people for whom I particularly intercede. Most of what distresses me is simply unknown to them. One of our local parishes invited John Spong[2] to town. I was riled, I was distressed, I was roused to apologetic zeal

---

2. The Rt. Rev. John Spong, formerly bishop of Newark and famously revisionist in his teachings which include frank denials of personal theism and the doctrine of the Incarnation. See John Shelby Spong, *Why Christianity Must Change or Die*.

On Being a Priest in a Difficult Time

and the defense of the true faith. We had a few folk who went to Spong's lecture. They didn't stay to be part of the new and improved Christianity. Most of the folk in my parish had no idea what the controversy was about. They were too preoccupied with the sick spouse, their drug-addicted child, the recent lay off, their own struggle to find the bare essentials of faith.

Within the parish, I live very much in the church into which I was ordained, and I exercise a ministry that has a form that is recognizably the same as the ministry exercised by the nine rectors before me in the 260 year history of the parish. It is when I am with other clergy, in the conventions and conventicles of our church, that I am forced to confront militant unbelief and unfaithfulness and moral relativism. I have these things in the parish but even their practitioners do not want to advertise or advance them. I find myself wondering how to raise and handle the issues of the "difficult times," that seem so irrelevant to the real difficulties of the real people for whom I pray, hoping and praying that God will sustain us all in our several callings. If I were to resign from the parish over some action of the General Convention, many people are likely to understand only that one particular intercessor has stopped praying for them. I need very much a way to stay with my parishioners without seeming to stand for things that are contrary to the vows I have taken.[3]

---

3. Since this essay was written I have affiliated with the Communion Partners, an organization of bishops, clergy, and parishes committed to staying loyal to both the Episcopal Church and the Anglican Communion.

15

Are Ordinations and Celebrations of New Ministry Too Elaborate?

THERE IS A CRITICISM that is often heard in our church these days that ordinations are too elaborate. The ceremonies and festivities that surround an ordination or the celebration of a new ministry are thought to imply an inappropriate significance for Holy Orders. If I may put words in the mouths of the critics, the complaint is that, "After all, baptism is the central and most important fact of Christian life. It is through baptism that one becomes a Christian and through baptism that the church reconstitutes its life. The ministry of the baptized is the fundamental ministry, and the ministry of the ordained is to be servants of the servants of God. By elaborate ordinations and celebrations of new ministry we give the impression that ordination is more important than baptism, that the clergy are the real Christians. Our ordination and institution ceremonies reinforce an outmoded clericalism, have distasteful overtones of authoritarianism, and undermine the ministry of the laity. Look at the Celebration of New Ministry in the Prayer Book. The people give the new priest a Bible, stoles, Prayer Books. In the end nothing is left. Everything has been given away."

This is the complaint, as I have often heard it, from some laity, clergy, bishops, seminary professors and deans. Drastic remedies are proposed: simplifying the rite, insisting on austerity, prohibitions against parties and special music. Some suggest having the laity join in the laying on of hands. Others suggest that the clergy should give gifts to the laity symbolic of the ministry of the baptized.

Are Ordinations and Celebrations of New Ministry Too Elaborate?

I believe that the ordination rites of the Book of Common Prayer are sound, that the form for the Celebration of New Ministry is wholesome, and that the ceremonies, enthusiasms, and piety which typically attend these events in the life of our church are a sign of hope. It is my conviction that our problem is not that we make too much of ordinations, but rather that both cleric and people too soon and too easily forget that for which they prayed.

There is one aspect of this criticism which I would like to affirm. In many parishes, one never sees a baptismal rite which begins to compare in grandeur with an ordination or the welcoming ceremony for a new rector. The problem is not that ordinations are too elaborate. The problem is that baptisms are often not celebrated with suitable dignity and grace. The Great Vigil of Easter is the normative baptismal feast. Three other major feasts of the Christian year are provided as alternatives. It is the perfunctory baptism of a child of a family with only a tangential relationship to the parish and a less than obvious commitment to the life of faith that diminishes the significance of baptism!

There is a problem here of liturgical practice. The problem is a neglect of the great feasts of the Christian year and a lack of understanding on the part of many church people of the meaning of the feasts. For this the clergy must bear a very great part (but not all) of the responsibility. The problem is not too much celebration at ordinations but not enough celebration at baptisms. In many places there are too few baptisms that the entire parish community can celebrate with enthusiasm and integrity. It is hard to get excited about a private family affair imposed on the congregation, especially when one may never see the family again.

When a man or woman after long preparation, thorough testing, and the approval of the entire church represented in all its orders, gives himself or herself to Christ in Holy Orders for the sake of the Church and the Church's mission to bring God's salvation to the world, those present in direct proportion to the degree that they take their own baptism seriously will give thanks, glorify God, and rejoice. They will feel their own faith and calling confirmed, and go with a full heart to the party afterward. There are no neo-puritanical liturgical reforms that can stop this natural movement of the human heart, in which, I dare say, God is well pleased.

If the clergy are simply functionaries, hirelings of the congregation (as so much of our policy implies with its contracts, work units, and extra-canonical job descriptions), then the ordination rites are too elaborate. But if there is a ministry of the Gospel and the Gospel sacraments, a ministry of stewarding Apostolic truth and practice, a ministry of "spiritual jurisdiction," a ministry of guarding the faith from soul-destroying error, a ministry of calling the Church to reconstitute itself in repentance, in a more total baptismal identity, as a more authentic Eucharistic community, a ministry entrusted to the Apostles and in succeeding generations to those who in their turn have been called, then all the people of God are bound to treat with great joy and celebration the moment when a person enters upon that sacred ministry.

They are bound to rejoice because in this ordination, Christ touches His Church and gives to the whole people of God that for which they hunger: "Bishops and other ministers who both by their life and doctrine set forth Thy true and lively Word, and rightly and duly administer Thy Holy Sacraments." Because of this ministry, the baptized have more than an individual conscience, more than the popular movements of the moment. They have clergy who are sworn and dedicated to faithfully transmit the teaching of the Apostles, and who are promised God's grace to carry out this ministry, in spite of the fact that this treasure is conveyed in earthen vessels.

This is a very beautiful thing. It is not more beautiful than baptism. But without the election and consecration of successors to the Apostles, baptism into a truly catholic, universal church is not possible. The faith into which one is baptized will become merely what is here now, instead of what has always and ever been. The baptism of babies and the consecration of bishops are both beautiful and poignant because they are the means by which the saving action of Christ is extended to the next generation. The Church will naturally surround both events with beauty and ceremony. There need be no feeling that to honor the one is to diminish the other. However, the consecration of a bishop is the means by which the Church reconstitutes itself as a baptizing community, able to baptize people in the faith of the Apostles, able to baptize into the church catholic, the church universal. The consecration of a bishop touches all the parishes, all the dioceses, other churches. It appropriately means more to more people and will naturally be celebrated with a devotion which is incommensurate with a local baptism. This does not diminish the dignity of baptism but it shows what a great thing it is into which one is being baptized.

The beauty of the ordination rites is about the only thing we have to save Holy Orders from becoming a mundane job. It might seem to some that the cleric as employee would be a relief from a church in which too

Are Ordinations and Celebrations of New Ministry Too Elaborate?

much is made of clergy and too little of the ministry of the people. Making ordinations and services of installation more mundane, more matter-of-fact will have the consequence of also making the ministry of laity more mundane and less awesome. The trend of the last twenty-five years of secularizing our understanding of the clergy role has done little to make the people of God more holy or more empowered in their baptismal ministry, and it has done much to reinforce the very clericalism (the priest does the ministry, the people receive and evaluate it) that is so deplored.

It is an essential role of those in holy orders to continually call the baptized to a greater recognition of the dignity of each person's calling and to support and uphold the baptized in that calling. Surely, the ministry whose service is, in season and out, to call the Church to repentance and holiness, to proclaim God's mercy, grace, and will to abundantly give that holiness, must have an appropriate dignity or be very hampered in fulfilling its calling.

There is also at work in these criticisms a very Puritan understanding of power. The Anabaptists did the wrong thing for the right reason: in response to magical, superstitious understandings of the sacraments, the Puritans robbed the sacraments of all mystical, supernatural power and made them merely symbolic and memorial. For Puritans, ordination is removed from the sacramental world altogether and becomes the conveying of institutional authority. The minister has an authority of office conveyed by the congregation. This was not the wish of all the non-Lutheran Reformers, but in practice their nuanced theories of ordination give way before the obvious political metaphors. If Christ is not really present to the Church in a unique way in the Eucharist, it is not conceivable that there is a unique presence of Christ for the Church through holy orders.

Political metaphors of power have come to dominate the discussion of ecclesiology. It is true enough that the Church is a human and political institution. As such, the Church is liable to the uses and abuses of power of all such institutions. The founders of the Episcopal Church were well aware of this and filled our constitution with checks and balances. There is nothing wrong with a political analysis of the Church. However, if that is where we stop, we are left with an understanding of the power relationships between clergy and laity based on a zero sum game. Political power is seen as a power pie. If you have power, it is because you have taken a larger slice of pie, which means my slice is smaller. That kind of power is real. It can be dangerous and addictive, to the laity as well as the clergy. In many parish churches, it is as likely to be wielded by a lay pope as by an authoritarian rector. I believe that our constitution and canons are up to the challenge of these power dynamics, if priest and parish will each accept the appropriate constitutional canonical roles. (The current penchant for tinkering with the constitution of the Episcopal Church by a generation that is naive about and unlettered in such things compared to the eighteenth century is tragedy in the making.)

There is another kind of power that is miraculous, mysterious, and abundantly fecund. For this kind of power, the more I have, the more you have, and the more you have, the more I have. This is the mystical power of Christ to which the Church has many avenues of access, including the avenue of holy orders. If the people have not power in their ministry, if they are not progressing in holiness and service, it is likely that the ministry of their priest lacks mystical power. One cause may be that the priest is not dwelling in his or her holy order and claiming the promised grace of God. Indeed, something is always lacking in our surrender to our vocation, be it clerical or lay. It can be the priest's relation to the reality of his or her vocation that causes a lack of power. It can also be that the people will not empower the priest, that they will insist that he or she have no power but whatever is given over to accomplish the projects of the moment. It may be that the people diminish the office of priest and the promise made by Christ to grace His Church through that office. If we thus turn our pastors into hirelings, the wolf will come, because the wolf knows that the hireling will flee. A merely functional, organizational, political understanding of holy orders devoid of sacramental power leaves us with only the personality of the cleric and his or her natural abilities. This is a formula for bitter disappointment for people and clergy alike. When the dimension of the mystical presence of Christ to the Church through holy orders is lost, the dignity and holiness of the ministry of the baptized will be lost as well! When the sacramental, mystical understanding of holy orders becomes diminished, the real power of the laity to follow Christ is impoverished.

If ordinations and installations are seen primarily as events through which Christ gifts the whole church with a unique mode of His presence by providing continuing Apostolic teaching, preaching, and sacramental leadership, there will be no need to feel that anything is being taken from the people. The tokens they give are meant to convey their prayers that the poor man or woman through whom Christ intends to gift His church will cooperate with this mysterious working of the Holy Spirit for the building

Are Ordinations and Celebrations of New Ministry Too Elaborate?

up of the whole church. Let us have noble, joyous, and solemn baptisms, whenever possible on Easter Eve, wherever possible done by the Bishop. Let us have noble, joyous, solemn consecrations, ordinations, and institutions. At ordinations and institutions, let the Bishop present tokens of ministry appropriate for the Bishop to present and let the people present tokens appropriate for the people to present. Let us refrain from taking liberty with the forms and adding gifts and tokens that do not celebrate the gift Christ is giving His Church in clergy who "both by their life and doctrine set forth Thy true and lively Word, and rightly and duly administer Thy holy sacraments."

16

Ontology or Function?: Thoughts on the Anniversary of My Ordination

IN THE CHURCH, MINISTRY, and Sacraments class at Trinity School for Ministry, we spent one three-hour session on the theology of ordination. The hoary question of whether ordination is a functional reality or an ontological reality was hotly debated by the students with surprisingly strong feelings on both sides. Strong Evangelicals hear the language of ontological change as a claim to a superior and super-holy status with magical powers. It sounds superstitious and magical and the worst sort of works righteousness to them. The more catholic-minded hear the functional language as a denial of any real change made in the individual by the power of the sacrament and as an understanding of the ordained ministry that has no way of comprehending the mystical dimension of holy orders. Functional language sounds secular and earthbound in catholic ears.

The terms of the debate are the terms of the polemic that has developed since the Reformation. On the Reform side, the rejection of any notion of ontological change has been driven by a desire to foreclose any possibility of an opening for works righteousness. On the catholic side, the upholding of the ontological language is driven by a desire to honor the power and grace of God working sacramentally in the church, and by the desire to honor the irrevocable nature of God's call and action in making a person a priest of the church.

To say that there is an ontological change in the ordinand is not necessarily to say that the person is super-holy or has magical powers. It is simply to say that a real change has taken place, that the person will never

Ontology or Function?: Thoughts on the Anniversary of My Ordination

be, can never be the same again. The person may be a good priest, a bad priest, a spoiled priest, but never again someone who has not made these promises and had hands laid upon them and been set apart by the prayer of the church for the ministry of word and sacrament. Something real has happened. To deny this seems to deny both the reality of human action and of God's action. To say as Evangelicals are wont to do that ordination is the empowering of the Holy Spirit for specific functions in the church sounds in the end very much like an ontological change. For how is it that vows are made and the Spirit poured out and nothing real and irrevocable happens?

I remember very powerfully my own ordination. I was ordained on the Feast of Pentecost, June 7, 1981, in St. Anne's Church in Mars Hill, Maine. The little church had been a chicken house that was moved across the town and set on a little hill overlooking Route One. The church was beautified by being lined with pressed tin on the walls and ceilings. I had always imagined being ordained in a beautiful Cathedral and my ordination was more beautiful than I could have imagined.

The church was packed. We had over a hundred and twenty people in this small building that had seating for maybe fifty. There were two dozen clergy, everything from Baptists to Roman Catholics. Most of the Anglican clergy present were from Canada and there was one priest from the Church of Sweden who was serving the Lutheran congregation in New Sweden. He was invited by the bishop to join in the laying on of hands.

There was a tremendous wind blowing that day and it was very warm and all the windows of the church were open. We were also in the middle of an army worm outbreak and the roads were slick with the bodies of the migrating worms. The worms had denuded many of the trees. The landscape was devastated and exquisitely beautiful at the same time.

The little church had a small sacristy in which there was a mirror. Two dozen clergy were taking turns before the mirror trying to look presentable. Hair provided a particular challenge. The heat and the dry wind blowing through the church created abundant static electricity, causing everyone's hair to stand on end. Of course the more you tried to comb your hair down the more it stood up. The clergy clustered around the one mirror trying to get presentable. I remember being especially anxious about it and very frustrated that I couldn't get my hair to lie down.

The priest that sponsored me for ordination was a bit of a holy fool and could always be counted on to do the unexpected. While we all stood jostling in front of the mirror, he came into the sacristy and pulled his hair straight up until it literally crackled with electricity. With an ecstatic expression on his face, Fr. Watson said, "This is what it was like on the first Pentecost!" We were stunned, and then he reached his hand out to touch me and a spark a hand's breadth wide jumped from him to me and I was shocked in more than ways than one.

I remember so much from that day, the smell of the incense, the people, the reverence of the two boys who were the acolytes. (One is now a teacher and the other a physician's assistant.) I remember signing the ordination document and making my subscription. I had prayed and thought hard about this, working my way through in particular to being able to profess the resurrection of the body with the conviction necessary for the one ordained to lead the people in their profession of faith. I remember the bishop vesting himself just before the laying on of hands in tunicle, dalmatic, and chasuble, and I remember being overwhelmed by a perception of the fullness of the Church as a sacred mystery, of the body of Christ pouring down upon us from antiquity and streaming out before us into eternity.

Then there was the laying on of hands. The physical pressure was immense. I had been prepared for it and was ready but it took real strength to bear the weight of the hands upon my head. At the prayer of ordination I was shot through with the most holy fear, right through from head to foot. Indeed it is a fearful thing to fall into the hands of the living God.

I was ordained with all the Anglo-Catholic ceremony. After being vested, my hands were anointed with chrism and bound together with a stole in a posture of prayer with the thumbs free. A Bible was placed on my hands and I gripped it with my thumbs. Then a chalice and paten were placed there and I gripped them. It could not be more clear that my life from henceforth was to be tied to the ministry of Word and sacrament. I looked down at my bound hands and thought, "perfect freedom is to be the slave of Jesus Christ."

The service went on and I shared the canon of the Eucharist with the bishop. We processed out of the church and stood by the door. I was quite overcome with emotion and put my hands to my face. The smell of the oil was strong and a balm and I breathed it in. I was dimly aware of someone calling my name and I spread my hands just a bit and looked down to see the bishop kneeling at my feet. "May I have your blessing, Father." I was completely undone and utterly humbled. It was at that moment that the reality of ordination came thundering in upon me. I was nothing, had nothing, had done nothing, could do nothing but hang on to Him and

Ontology or Function?: Thoughts on the Anniversary of My Ordination

pronounce His blessing and marvel at the calling and promises of God. One by one every person in the congregation knelt for an individual blessing. It was as if something were being hammered into my soul. It was death and then dying again and again and again. I cried all the tears I had before the end of the line of people came. I thought I couldn't go on and I did. Pure grace. Really the whole ministry was there in those few minutes. "A broken and contrite heart, I will not despise." It was as they say real.

God grant it shall be so to the end of my days. One can only marvel at the treasures that God conveys through earthen vessels and broken hearts.

17

Administering the Ashes on Ash Wednesday 2009

I WAS ONE OF the priests administering ashes today in chapel at the school. I also gave out the bread at Communion. I will be doing the same in a local parish tonight. There are things that I do in the priesthood that routinely break my heart. Person after person comes and quietly submits to having ashes imposed on their forehead and takes away with them these words, "Remember you are dust and to dust you shall return." It seems to me that each person comes wrapped in their own death, in the mortality we all bear and that we choose at least in this moment not to flee, and wrapped also in the dying that is unique to their particular life. It is part of pastoral ministry even in a school that you inevitably know something of the particular dying each person brings. Each one brings perhaps a long struggle with a chronic illness, a losing battle with persistent depression, a sick child, the recent loss of a parent, the shame of constant defeat in the battle with a besetting sin. I don't know the whole story but enough of each one that my heart is pierced through with the beauty of their faithful burden-bearing and their hope that Christ will touch, forgive, and heal. I have much the same perception and the same feeling each time I administer the bread and wine at Holy Communion.

I have become more and more suspicious of the concept of the nominal Christian. Our parish churches are supposed to be full of nominal Christians who are just going through the motions, of half-believers who are relying on their good works, and who have not really surrendered to Christ and accepted the Gospel. In any parish church there are a few real apostates, and a few real scoffers, and perhaps a few who genuinely hate God. Their numbers are routinely exaggerated. Most of the people who come to the church Sunday by Sunday know they are dying and are placing their hope in Christ. It may be an inarticulate hope, it may be a confused hope. Often there are huge brambles of misunderstanding that must be cleared away before the whole power of the good news can come in upon them. Often there is real darkness into which the light of Christ has not yet come, that cries out for a light-bearer. Yet, they come. When Jesus saw such as these gathered in their multitudes on the hill side, the sight provoked in him not contempt for the nominal but compassion, "for they were like sheep without a shepherd" (Matt 9:36, Mark 6:34).

I give thanks to God for those who come to have ashes put on their foreheads today even if they don't really know why they come, even if they cannot give an account of the hope that is in them. I give thanks to God who in Christ draws all people to Himself, and for His drawing power in the liturgy of the church, and I pray for the grace to communicate the living Christ to hearts and minds as I put the living bread in outstretched hands.

18

The Priesthood and Parish Conflict[1]

My experience with parish conflict: I have been ordained for twenty years and have led four parishes, of which three have had a history of conflict. I was a diocesan consultant in Maine and Massachusetts, and spent over a year working in one highly conflicted parish in which fist fights had been a feature of previous parish meetings. I was an early advocate of applying Family Systems Theory to parish life before this perspective was made famous by Edwin Friedman's great book. As an adjunct professor, I taught Family Theory and Therapy at Andover Newton Theological School and was a supervisor of field education supervisors at Episcopal Divinity School. I participated in an ongoing group for veterans of extreme parish conflict held at the Episcopal Divinity School in 1992 and 1993. Of the dozen or so members, including a bishop who was forced to resign his see, I was the only person who ultimately stayed in place and continued in office.

Learnings from my experience and from the survivors group. Most of the parishes of the members of the group were known to have a history of conflict before we arrived and often had a history of involuntary terminations. Many of these parishes had outstanding problems associated with membership and financial decline that had not been resolved and were not the primary topic of conflict. Often we felt these parishes were lacking in spirituality or theological integrity. We were often perceived as being "hard-nosed" for trying to promote minimal standards for vestry service (church attendance) or administration of the sacraments (preparation meetings). Interestingly, frequently the conflict flared up when the parish

---

1. This was a report prepared for the bishops of Connecticut, Nov. 24, 2004.

was growing in both numbers and finances. In many cases where the clergy resigned for "the good of the parish," the conflict continues. By the time we were meeting in our group, some of the parishes involved were already moving toward involuntary termination with our successors.

Most of the parishes of members of the group had difficult interims and the interim process was often a source of conflict. In many cases, the interim ministry was unskilled, untrained, and unsupervised. Often the rectors we replaced were larger than life figures with a great deal of personal charisma. When first introduced as the rector of our parish many of us were told that we didn't look the part. These parishes were often characterized as being very dependent on the personality of the rector and often were perceived to have faltered when the previous rector left. Often the leave-taking of the beloved former rector had not been emotionally appropriate, and had often been sudden or abrupt.

A sensitive issue that emerged was the role of substance abuse by previous clergy and key lay leaders in many of these parishes. Many of the members of our group were either in recovery or adult children of alcoholics or had other formative experiences of abuse and trauma as children. Many of us felt that there was a certain psychology of the victim at work. After being publicly berated and humiliated, we found ourselves ashamed and secretive, often not reaching out to people who could help us and often blamed for causing our own problems when we did. We found that we were often making decisions not on the basis of our cherished beliefs and values but on the basis of how to avoid being beaten up in public again.

Previous parish experience and advanced training were not good indicators of the potential for the ability to survive and thrive in these highly conflicted situations. Most of us were experienced and had been recommended on the basis of having the skills and experience to "handle" this kind of parish. Most of us had been successful and effective in other positions and had often managed parish conflict well. Before encountering the particular parish that brought us to the group, many of us felt that, though parish conflict could be very difficult, it could be managed with the right tools and approach. "Everything that worked before, didn't work here," was a refrain in our group.

Though the members of the group represented a broad spectrum of theological opinion, we all felt that we had moments when *we encountered spiritual evil in a way that we had not experienced it before.* We all agreed that the experience deepened our sense of dependence on God and our prayer life. Those of us who stayed in spite of requests for our resignation all felt in different ways that we were called by God to do so.

The intervention of the diocese and consultants in many cases made things worse rather than better. In highly conflicted parishes, consultants that were highly competent and experienced made what they admitted were "dumb" mistakes. In these highly anxious systems competent people often became incompetent. Our reflection was that most consultation models are mediation models or negotiation models. This is a model that works well with in a relatively stable situation when people of fundamentally good will disagree over some objective content. One of the features of these conflicts was that it was very difficult to uncover an objective content to the conflict. Our antagonists often could not articulate specific complaints or specific desired actions or corrections. The interim priest of a famous New York parish which has recently pushed out its rector commented when asked about the parish that "the vestry had no idea what it wanted and would stop at nothing to get it."

A useful distinction is made by Kenneth Haugk in his book, Antagonists in The Church[2], *between conflict for which mediation is appropriate and conflict for which adjudication is appropriate.* There is some conflict that is driven by emotional and spiritual pathology and is not amenable to negotiation. Perhaps the most famous example of someone misreading the nature of conflict in this way is the British prime minister, Chamberlain at the Munich Conference with Hitler. The end game that led to final resignation often included a number of steps the purpose of which was to appease the antagonists. They usually wanted more. The very presence of the consultants on site often seemed to embolden the antagonists. Often processes that were set up to facilitate communication were "hijacked" by antagonists who engaged in "get out the vote campaigns" while the supporters of the clergy were often not aware of what was going on. Often we were counseled by bishops and consultants to "take the high road" and not attempt in any organized way to rally our support. This was often a source of great anger and bitterness to our supporters when we left or resigned. "I had no idea what was going on," or "I wish someone had talked to me," were refrains that we heard from supporters after the event.

It is sometimes appropriate to use the canons; the system can work. In most cases, we were counseled to avoid the canonical process at all costs. Resignation of the rector was seen by many consultants and bishops as a

---

2. Haugk, *Antagonists in the Church*.

last resort that was still to be preferred to enacting the canonical process. We were warned that if we invoked the canons we "had already lost," and that "even if you win canonically, you will not be able to govern the parish afterwards." I am convinced that this was bad advice and that much like the Watergate episode in American political history, a crisis which can be resolved by the rule of law has a role in restoring faith in the integrity of the institution and the office involved. It is good for people and bad for bullies when the rules are understood and uniformly enforced. Rather than being morale destroying, there are times when invocation of the rule of law can be morale building, and actually lay a foundation for a better community life going forward.

It takes extensive, overlapping support systems to survive and overcome in severely conflicted parishes. I had a spiritual director, therapist, organizational coach, and several support groups. I also found solidarity in prayer with other clergy vital.

Suggestions for Action

Establish an early warning system. The diocese already has an ordinands training program that provides an opportunity to be in touch with new clergy who may be experiencing parish conflict as they start their careers. It might be helpful to establish two additional groups. There could be a group for clergy that are leaving their cures that could provide mutual support, encouragement, and training in best practices for a good close to a term of ministry. This group should cover at least the last three months of ministry. Another group would be for clergy of whatever stage of experience that were taking up a new cure. This should cover at least the first year to eighteen months.

Trained interims are not necessary in all transitions but in parishes with a long history of conflict there is a need for well trained and well supported interims. The amount of support and supervision people working in such an environment need is roughly equivalent to the clinical supervision needed by a therapist working with a severely troubled family or with borderline personalities; in other words, a lot of debriefing time off site with an experienced, wise, and spiritually grounded colleague.

Continuing supervision for the new rectors in troubled parishes by supervisors who have psychological and organizational skill and who have spiritual depth. Catching conflict early and intervening with skilled off site coaching of the clergy and at times key lay leaders appears to me more effective than sending in the "mission impossible team" at a later date. On site consulting often moves conflict in these parishes to a higher level.

A clear message which permeates the diocesan system that clergy can be terminated for good cause but that unless it involves moral failure, such terminations are rare and costly.

Establish a norm for lay leader training where lay people can receive meaningful Christian catechesis and formation, learn about the polity of the church, come to understand diocesan vision, values, and policy, and learn necessary skills, like conflict management and how to appropriately handle antagonists in the church.

Do anything which will raise awareness about the problem of substance abuse in parishes and which will help the many clergy who have grown up as over-responsible children in alcoholic or other kinds of turbulent families understand how that experience might be affecting their ministry.

Continue to keep an emphasis on spiritual growth and development. Emotional health, spiritual health, and organizational health are interrelated.

19

What is the Essence of the Episcopacy?

THERE IS A STANDARD form of the argument about the significance of episcopacy for the order of the church. Is episcopacy of the *esse, bene esse,* or *plene esse* of the church? That is, is episcopacy of the essence of the order of the church, so that without bishops in apostolic succession there is no church? Or is episcopacy essential for the good order of the church but not absolutely necessary? Or is episcopacy for the fullness of the order of the church, meaning that a church can be a valid church without bishops but that to be the fullness of the apostolic church demands the fullness of the apostolic order. The center of Anglican witness has been in the last two positions with a minority Anglo-Catholic report holding out for the first position. The great book about all of this is Michael Ramsey's *The Gospel and the Catholic Church*. Ramsey's argument fits perhaps best into the category of *plene esse*. Churches without bishops are certainly valid members of the body of Christ, but there is something about the fullness of the apostolic witness and unity that is lacking and toward which the churches should press with full vigor for the sake of a fuller and more adequate witness to the crucified and risen Lord. Ramsey's book convinced the Reformed pastor and missionary in India, Lesslie Newbigin, of the significance of the catholic order of the church for the sake of Gospel mission, and made it possible for Newbigin to embrace a call to be one of the first bishops of the Church of South India. Ramsey's book remains a classic and breaks open stale arguments by arguing for the evangelical and missionary significance of the catholic order of the church. It is a travesty that the book was so long out of print. If you ever see a used copy, buy it.

The moment of foment and crisis that we are enduring in the Anglican world brings to the fore the significance of the office of bishop. All the old questions about how or whether bishops are of the *esse* of the church are bound to arise anew. But at the same time, let us pause to ask what is of the *esse* of this order? What is essential to the office and ministry of the bishop? Ramsey argued that the bishop had an evangelical significance, for the bishop, like the apostles from which the office derived, was a living witness to the dependence of the whole body upon its one head and therefore upon the actual historical events of the crucifixion and resurrection of the Lord. The bishop was to hand on the tradition of the Apostles which was a witness to the life, death, and resurrection of the Lord.

A full answer to the question of what is of the *esse* of the episcopacy would take many pages. But a quick answer can be given here. Two things at least, that are completely interrelated and interdependent, are essential to the office of the bishop. One is the stewardship of apostolic doctrine. John Spong has written somewhere of the bishop as an "apostolic pioneer." Such a phrase is an oxymoron. Paul is quintessentially apostolic and laying out the essence of the apostolic order which the episcopacy must maintain if it is indeed to be an apostolic succession, when he says to the Corinthians, " I pass on to you that which I received, that the Lord Jesus on the night in which he was betrayed took bread. . . ." (1 Cor 11:23). To be a successor to the apostles is to hand on a witness which is primarily a report of things which God has done. To be a bishop is to be a sacred historian and the teller of a true witness and a true story. My word for this is to say that the bishop must be a faithful steward of apostolic doctrine. It is this witness which creates the one body utterly dependent on its one head and on the actual death and resurrection of the Lord.

Related to the ministry of stewardship of apostolic doctrine is the ministry of guarding the unity of the church. This is a unity in faith which is a response to the one witness, now mediated by the succession of teachers, to the one savior. The bishop is a visible link with the college of apostolic witnesses. The original twelve have a common witness, and witness to each other and the church and the waiting world that their witness is authentic and true just because it is a common witness. The apostles and their successors in the apostolic ministry of bishops are to build up the one church in unity for the sake of its mission of bringing all the nations to the worship of the one true and living God within the body of Christ. It is of the essence of the episcopal office that the bishop cultivates and guards the unity of the church. This places a heavy responsibility on those in episcopal office to keep faith with the apostolic teachers that have preceded them and to be servants of ecumenical solidarity. Thus the bishops are to be living sacraments of the unity of the body of Christ.

20

Godly Bishops

IN WHAT FOLLOWS I am going to take it as established that the historic episcopacy is a continuation of the apostolic ministry which has evolved in the Church under the guidance of the Holy Spirit, and that therefore an episcopacy which has integrity and authenticity will be self-consciously seeking an ever greater conformity with the ministry of the first Apostles.

One way of speaking about godliness in the episcopacy would be to enumerate all the virtues that would go into a truly consecrated character. So we would speak of prayerfulness, learning, humility, the spirit of service, zeal for souls, and so on. But how might a bishop find a way into these virtues? How can the motivation to grow in real godliness be sustained? I think by dwelling on the originating encounter with the crucified and risen Lord which propels the Apostles into their ministry. Essential to the ministry of the first Apostles is that they are witnesses to the resurrection; it is in the resurrection encounters that we should expect to find the distinctive shape and power of the apostolic ministry.

Three locations dominate my thinking, meditation, and prayer about the apostolic office. First there is John 20:19–23. The apostles are cowering behind closed doors, and the crucified and risen one appears to them. He shows them his hands and his side. They are glad when they see the Lord and he then says to them, "Peace be with you, As the Father has sent me even so I send you." Then the Lord breathes on them and says, "Receive the Holy Spirit. If you forgive the sins of any, they are forgiven; if you retain the sins of any, they are retained." To be an Apostle is to be one who is sent. Jesus is the Apostle of the Father, and in his turn the crucified and risen one sends out his own apostles, whose mission is to create by their witness a community of witness to the crucified and risen Lord and to the presence of his Spirit. At the heart of this witness is the extension of the reconciliation which has been offered to them. That the Apostles are given the authority to proclaim the reality of reconciliation and to distinguish false from true reconciliation is not some arbitrary power but a personal authority and knowledge that comes from their own actual personal redemption and what they have learned from welcoming and embracing the one who comes to breathe into them God's peace.

The apostolic ministry originates in a personal encounter with the savior. There is no way for these original witnesses to claim their vocation without looking upon the one whom they have betrayed and abandoned. They cannot be reconciled to him who holds out his wounded and glorified hands without embracing their own faithlessness and sinfulness. This dynamic is portrayed even more starkly in the encounter between Jesus and Peter on the beach in the twenty-first chapter of St. John's Gospel. Peter rushes to the beach where the Lord meets him over a charcoal fire and asks those excruciating questions, "Peter, do you love me?" There by that charcoal fire Peter must think of another interrogation and of his betrayal of the Lord. Peter can only answer the call to go and gather and feed the sheep by embracing the fire of his own sin. The connection between a personal confession of sin and the reception of the call to gather in and feed the flock of Christ that is being driven home to Peter on the beach in Galilee is there as well behind those closed doors in Jerusalem. The reception of the crucified and risen one's commission to go and tell the nations begins necessarily with a personal sense of sinfulness and failure which is provoked by the sudden breaking in of the undeserved forgiveness of God. I am not speaking so much of a particular type of conversion experience but of the reality of knowing oneself as a betrayer and crucifier of the Lord, and knowing oneself as the recipient of an undeserved and costly forgiveness. There is a place where shame and joy grow together, where a growing consciousness of the enormity of human sin and rebellion and a consciousness of the astonishing goodness of the seeking, searching, sacrificial love of God grow together. In this place that is at once a place of deep humiliation and deep peace, the words of the Lord "even so I send you" can be rightly heard, and when heard are an irresistible invitation to return love for love. Here the human race is being remade by a new genesis, a new inspiration of God's Spirit. From this place the forgiveness of sins can be declared and the lost sheep of the Father gathered in. Here is the wellspring of godliness in

To Persevere in Love

the ministry of bishop and shepherd. The way into this place is the way of humility, of lowliness, and of deepening repentance.

The third scriptural location I propose is suggested to me by Lesslie Newbigin. It is Paul's encounter with the crucified and risen Lord on the road to Damascus, recorded in Acts 9. Paul is a persecutor of the church of God and is thrown to the ground by his encounter with the Lord. Lying in the dust, he hears the Lord say to him, "Saul, why are you persecuting me?" Here we have the same revelation of sinfulness and of utterly undeserved love and forgiveness which strips Paul of any righteousness of his own. The disciples in Jerusalem, Peter on the beach, and Paul on the road all share in the same humiliation which is at once an exaltation, in the same death which is at once life. In Paul's circumstance, an aspect of this originating apostolic encounter is made especially clear. In order to embrace his call to be an apostle, Paul must not only confess himself as God's enemy but in order to grasp the wounded and glorified hand stretched out to him, Paul must also grasp the hands of those he has persecuted. Paul must recognize the nascent church as the body of Christ. Paul cannot be reconciled to God without being reconciled to God's people. Paul recognizes that God is building a new people which shall be marked off not by the works of the law but by faith in the crucified and risen Messiah. Paul recognizes that God's promise to recreate humanity, to reconcile the nations in a renewed Israel is coming true in and through Jesus. In Paul's call we learn that to be a witness to the resurrection is to be at one and the same time a witness to the reality of the new Israel which is the body of the Christ.

Just these few encounters we have considered point us to elements that are at the heart of the ministry of episcopacy, and if they are held fast, set a person on the same road toward holiness and godliness trod by the first Apostles. We learn that the apostolic ministry begins with a deep and personal apprehension of the forgiveness of sins by the crucified and risen Lord. Included in this forgiveness and reconciliation with God is the fact of the Church, the Body of Christ, and the new human life that comes in this encounter by the gift of the Spirit propels one into the life of mission, evangelization, and witness.

The witness and authority of the original Apostles is intensely personal. They stand before the world as men personally convicted and personally redeemed by their encounters with the crucified and risen Lord. It is possible for us to distinguish between the evangelical concern for personal faith and the catholic concern for the body of Christ and for the apostolic ministry as a vital organ in the body of Christ, but these elements are encountered in the Bible always simultaneously, inextricably intertwined. The first Apostles are living proof and a sacramental sign of the forgiveness of sins, the reconciliation with God, and the reality of the one body dependent on its one head, by their very presence. The message authenticates the person and the person authenticates the message. (It is of course possible for this relationship between person and message to be impaired; this is perhaps the source of ungodliness in episcopal ministry.)

We come to our encounter with the crucified and risen one through the testimony of these original witnesses as that testimony is transmitted to us through the Word of God and through the succession of apostolic teaching and witness. The challenge for the contemporary bishop who wishes to stand in the shoes of the original Apostles is to dwell in and upon the Word of God in such a way that this originating apostolic encounter becomes real and personal and having once found this originating moment of encounter to return to it again and again and let it be the engine of the bishop's teaching, preaching, and witness. This call to return again and again to the epicenter of the apostolic earthquake is a call to prayer and contemplation. It is a call to a life of study of the Bible and of the faithful teachers who by God's grace make a faithful succession to the Apostles possible. It is call to mission, to evangelization, to invite others into this encounter (which is bound to come in different ways for different people) with the crucified and risen Lord.

This call is also a call to guarding the unity of the church. The new life with God which the savior comes to bring us at so great a price is a new life with each other no less than with God. It is the restoration of God's plan that he should be our Father and we should be his children and loving brothers and sisters of each other. At the center of the apostolic experience of forgiveness is the reality of the one people of God and the body of Christ. The Apostles witness to the reality of the forgiveness of sins not just as an idea, as a teaching of the master, but as something that he has accomplished by his costly work, and that has now through the power of the resurrection and the gift of the Spirit appeared. The unity of the college of the apostles in witness and in love is part of the Gospel which they proclaim. The Bible already tells the sad story that this testimony can be marred by a lack of unity and by attempts to find the center of the church in anything other than the forgiveness of sins brought by the death and resurrection of the Lord. If the secret of godliness in the episcopacy is dwelling upon the personal invitation to confession and the personal offer of redemption given by the outstretched, wounded, and glorified hand of the risen one, then the bishop seeking godliness will want to lead the whole church back to this one cornerstone that it might be built up in unity and by the Spirit of love which is breathed by Christ into his church at just this point. There must be an impatience with anything which would seek to define the church on any other basis. There must be a resolute resistance to any attempt to draw the church away from utter dependence on the actual death and resurrection of her Lord. A godly bishop is one who stands in the center of the church as an authentic and personal sign of the reality of forgiveness and new life with God and among people that comes through the utter dependence of the whole church upon its one head and upon the actual events of the death and resurrection of the Lord.

21

Bearing the Word of God

John 17:11–19

To those who have a vocation to bear God's Word into the world

THE PEOPLE TO WHOM you are called to speak this word of Love have the same heart that you have and that I have. It is a heart that deeply and desperately wants this love, and it is a heart that is frightened. The very depth of our feeling frightens us. This fear leads us into those places where we have been abandoned and betrayed, into the wilderness. There the voice of the evil one speaks and says, "There is not enough for you. God will not take care of you but I will take care of you."

This voice releases rage, hostility and envy. Envy is the feeling that if I am hungry, it is because someone else is being fed. Envy says, if I cannot eat, no one will eat, and envy plots destruction.

There are people to whom you are being sent who have lived too long starved of God's love. They mistrust that there ever could be food and they do their best to still their pangs. If you are bearing the Word of Love and you offer it to others and they see others being nourished, they will be furious and attempt to destroy you and the people who are being fed. The person who brings the Word of Love will inevitably be tested, inevitably

To Persevere in Love

meet hostility. Inevitably your trust in the never-failing provision of the Good Shepherd will be sorely tested.

All of this happened to the Good Shepherd. We have ourselves tested God in this way. But the Risen One comes to us with the marks of the cross still upon him. Now we know that Love is so abundant that we cannot destroy it. Now He breathes His Spirit into us and we come to remorse and repentance for not coming to the banquet sooner. Now envy is spent. Now there is room at the table for brothers and sisters.

I pray you will meet hostility and envy with trust in the abundant love and provision of God. Do not listen to the voice of the Tempter. Persevere in Love. In this way shall there be at last one flock, one Shepherd. Amen.

Bibliography

Anglican/Roman Catholic International Commission. "A/RCIC Statement on the Doctrine of the Ministry." Canterbury: A/RC Joint Preparatory Commission, 1973. http://www.pro.urbe.it/dia-int/arcic/doc/e_arcic_ministry.html.

Church of England. *The Book of Common Prayer*:1662 *Version (includes Appendices from the* 1549 *Version and Other Commemorations)*. Everyman's Library 241. London: David Campbell, 1999.

Church Hymnal Corporation. *The Book of Common Prayer*. New York: Church Hymnal Corp., 1979.

Dickens, Charles. *The Annotated Christmas Carol*. Notes by Michael Hearn. New York: Crown, 1976.

Dulles, Avery. *Models of the Church*. Garden City: Doubleday, 1974, Image Books, 1987.

Eisner, Elliot W. *The Educational Imagination: On the Design and Evaluation of School Programs*. New York: Macmillan, 2nd ed., 1985.

Farrer, Austin. *Austin Farrer: The Essential Sermons*. J.L. Houlden, ed. London: SPCK, 1991.

Fenhagen, James C. *Ministry and Solitude: The Ministry of the Laity and the Clergy in Church and Society*. New York: Seabury, 1981.

———. *Mutual Ministry: New Vitality for the Local Church*. New York: Seabury, 1977.

Fenhagen, James C. and Celia A. Hahn. *Ministry for a New Time*. Washington, D.C.: The Alban Institute in cooperation with Cornerstone Foundation of the Episcopal Church Foundation, 1995.

Franklin, R. William, ed. *Anglican Orders: Essays on the Centenary of Apostolicae Curae, 1896–1996*. London: Mowbray, 1996.

Guthrie, Clifton F. *Sacral Power: A De-Centered Theology of Clergy Authority*. PhD diss., Emory University, 1996.

Harding, Leander S. "The Priesthood and the Center," originally published as "The Ministry and the Center" in *Story Lines: Chapters on Thought, Word, and Deed: For Gabriel Fackre*. Edited by Gabriel J. Fackre and Skye Fackre Gibson. Grand Rapids: Eerdmans, 2002. Reprinted by permission.

———. "The Power and Dignity of the Priesthood." In *Sewanee Theological Review* 43.2. Sewanee: The School of Theology, 2000. Reprinted by permission.

———. "What Have We Been Telling Ourselves about the Priesthood?" In *Sewanee Theological Review* 43.2. Sewanee: The School of Theology, 2000. Reprinted by permission.

Haugk, Kenneth C. *Antagonists in the Church: How to Identify and Deal with Destructive Conflict*. Minneapolis: Augsburg, 1988.

Bibliography

Herbert, George. *The Poetical Works of George Herbert*. Edited by the Rev. A.B. Grosart, LL.D. London: George Bell and Sons, 1903.

Holmes, Urban T., III. *The Expression of the Ineffable: The Dialogue Between Theology and Culture in Contemporary American Society*. PhD diss., Marquette University, 1972. Ann Arbor, MI: University Microfilms, 1972.

———. *The Future Shape of Ministry: A Theological Projection*. New York: Seabury, 1971.

———. *Ministry and Imagination*. New York: Seabury, 1976.

———. *The Priest in Community: Exploring the Roots of Ministry*. New York: Seabury, 1978.

———. *Spirituality for Ministry*. New York: Harper and Row, 1982.

Hooker, Richard. *The Folger Library Edition of the Works of Richard Hooker*. Cambridge, MA: Belknap Press of Harvard University Press, 1977.

John Paul II. *Crossing the Threshold of Hope*. Edited by Vittorio Messori. New York: Knopf; London: J. Cape, 1994.

Lightfoot, Joseph Barber. *Dissertations on the Apostolic Age: Reprinted from Editions of St. Paul's Epistles*. London, New York: Macmillan, 1892.

Moberly, Robert Campbell. *Ministerial Priesthood. Chapters (preliminary to a Study of the Ordinal) on the Rationale of Ministry and the Meaning of Christian Priesthood, with an Appendix upon Roman Criticism of Anglican Orders*. Ed. 2. London: John Murray, 1899.

Ramsey, Michael. *The Gospel and the Catholic Church*. Cambridge, MA: Cowley Classic Reprint, 1990, based on 2nd ed., New York: Longmans and Green, 1956.

Sloyan, Gerard S. Review of *Ministry and Imagination*, by Urban T. Holmes III. *Worship* 51.2 (March 1977): 167.

Spong, John Shelby. *Why Christianity Must Change or Die: A Bishop Speaks to Believers in Exile*. San Francisco: Harper, 1998.

White, Roger J. "Teachers and Evangelists for the Equipment of the Saints: Prayer Book Doctrine Concerning the Bishop as Teacher, Evangelist, and Focus of Unity." In *On Being a Bishop: Papers on Episcopacy from the Moscow Consultation, 1992*. Edited by J. Robert Wright. New York: Church Hymnal Corp., 1993.

Zabriskie, Stewart C. *Total Ministry: Reclaiming the Ministry of All God's People*. Washington DC: Alban Institute, 1995.